finding peace

finding peace

PRAYER JOURNAL
for Women

Weekly Devotions, Prompts & Exercises
for Managing Anxiety

HELEN H. LEE, MSc

ZEITGEIST • NEW YORK

Published in the United States by Zeitgeist, an imprint of Zeitgeist™, a division of Penguin Random House LLC, New York.
penguinrandomhouse.com

Zeitgeist™ is a trademark of Penguin Random House LLC.

Scripture quotations marked (KJV) are taken from the King James Version.

ISBN: 9780593435939

Cover and interior art © Shutterstock/vectortwins
Book design by Erin Yeung and Katy Brown

Printed in Mexico

1 3 5 7 9 10 8 6 4 2

First Edition

This book is dedicated to anyone who has ever felt alone and has experienced struggles with anxiety in their walk with God.

You are so loved.

Contents

Part One
PRAYER JOURNAL

Part Two

ANXIETY RELIEF EXERCISES

Introduction

I used to feel unsafe talking about my struggles with anxiety. Having anxiety made me feel that there was something wrong with me. Seeing others who looked like they had everything together, I felt a lot of shame. I felt alone, like I was the only one who was struggling.

As a child of immigrants, I felt the pressure of being perfect. I believed the only way I could be loved was meeting others' expectations of me. I relied on certain metrics, like academic performance and career success, to define my self-worth, and it caused me to experience emotional highs and lows. I struggled with depression and anxiety because my self-worth was defined by how well I performed on paper, and I never felt I could live up to what I thought was expected of me.

Even after I accepted Jesus as my Savior and knew He loved me, I still struggled. It was in this season of life that I began journaling. Journaling enabled me to process my thoughts and feelings as I wrote reflections about what I'd read in the Bible and the truths that I'd learned. Journaling helped me understand why I was full of anxiety and how I had been building my identity on the wrong things instead of as a daughter of God. As I learned more about God's attributes and my identity in Christ, I began to internalize that God's grace empowers me to live victoriously. Now, as a life coach, I can help other women navigate challenges by showing them how turning to God helped me and how He can help them too.

I've witnessed the power of journaling as a transformative tool that helps women internalize God's love. In a world full of distractions, a prayer journal can help us find perspective when we are plagued with fear and anxious thoughts.

This journal combines prayer with Scripture to help refocus your mind on God. God's Word has the power to transform us. Filled with essential truths, Scripture can be applied in any circumstance and can help us in any situation we encounter.

I hope that the time spent with this prayer journal fills your spiritual cup and empowers you to experience God's presence and receive His grace. Do not be discouraged if journaling does not come easily or naturally; it takes time to make it a practice. And remember that journaling is one of the many ways you can connect with God, and He is loving and patient.

TIPS FOR STAYING CONSISTENT

- Be intentional. Carve out time free from distractions.

- Be accountable. Record the times you journal on a habit tracker.

- Be gentle with yourself. No matter how many times you fall, you can always get back up.

- Be patient. Treat your journey as a marathon, not a sprint.

- Be humble. Lean on God's grace to do the heavy lifting.

Before You Get Started

The key features in this book will provide guidance for your prayer life and will help you intentionally use Scripture to combat anxiety. The weekly themes and selected biblical text will support you when you are feeling anxious.

Reading God's Word will remind you of the magnitude of His love and care for you. God knows what you are going through, your unique personality, and even the number of hairs on your head (Matthew 10:30). God knows you better than you know yourself!

This journal features thoughtful prompts that will help you reflect on the Scriptures provided. Study the reflections and uncover what God is trying to reveal to you, then use the prompts to help you apply God's lessons in your own intentions and writing.

TIPS TO GET THE MOST OUT OF JOURNALING:

- Take deep, slow breaths to quiet and calm your spirit before writing.

- Ask God for spiritual understanding and to remove any obstructions that may make it difficult to hear from Him.

- Be honest in your responses.

- Avoid censoring yourself or judging what you have written.

- If prompts are challenging to answer, write the first thoughts that come to mind or explore why on paper.

Anxiety Relief Exercises

Each week's devotion provides suggested exercises found in Part II of this book to help you apply the weekly theme to your day-to-day. Combining prayer and actionable solutions can help you overcome the worst of your anxiety and start living the life God wants for you.

TIPS FOR WRITING PRAYERS:

- Identify what promises or lessons you can take away from the Scripture.

- Ask God to reveal actionable steps for relieving anxiety symptoms.

- Talk to God honestly about what you think and feel. He will meet you where you are.

- Ask God to reveal clarity and objectivity about your situation.

- Trust in the Spirit to help guide you when you feel stuck and do not know what to pray about.

Part One

PRAYER
JOURNAL

Week 1

GOD MEETS YOU WHERE YOU ARE

"I waited patiently for the LORD; and he inclined unto me, and heard my cry. He brought me up also out of an horrible pit, out of the miry clay, and set my feet upon a rock, and established my goings."

PSALM 40:1–2

Anxiety can begin with one small worry. Then the "what-ifs" snow-ball, leading us to believe that something catastrophic is looming around the corner, and suddenly, panic sets in.

When anxiety engulfs us, it can feel like there is no way out. At the same time, our problems can seem too trivial for God to concern Himself with; however, as Psalm 40:1–2 says, no matter what level of anxiety we are experiencing, we can cry out to Him. Sometimes we may feel we need to get our act together before we can approach God. But God hears us even with our jumbled thoughts. He can lift us out of the pit and set us upon a rock, a stable foundation where He can direct and guide us.

I heard of a woman who, in the split moment before a car T-boned into her and her husband's car, called out to God in one frantic word, "Help!" God heard her, and despite the car being wrecked, they walked out of that horrible accident unscathed. The King of the universe turns to us and meets us where we are to hear our calls, no matter our state of mind.

ANXIETY RELIEF EXERCISE

Giving God Your Worries and Fears (page 207). This exercise will help you turn to God and share your fears and worries with Him. Know that He will turn to you and hear everything you have to say.

PRAYERS

God turns Himself toward us to help lift us out of despair. Have you experienced this in your life? If so, how were you encouraged by it?

What would you like to tell God the next time you begin to get swept up by an onslaught of anxious thoughts?

Day 1

_____

_____

_____

_____

_____

Day 2

_____

_____

_____

_____

_____

Day 3

_____

_____

_____

_____

_____

Day 4

_____
_____
_____
_____
_____

Day 5

_____
_____
_____
_____
_____

Day 6

_____
_____
_____
_____
_____

Day 7

_____
_____
_____
_____
_____

Week 2

BARE YOUR SOUL TO GOD

*"Why art thou cast down, O my soul? and why art thou
disquieted within me? hope in God: for I shall yet praise him,
who is the health of my countenance, and my God."*

PSALM 43:5

When we are entrenched in chaos, we are likely to experience discomfort. We question whether God sees us or whether He's rejected
us. Somewhere along the line, many of us have learned that our
honest feelings are an inconvenience to others, so we choose
to hide them. Putting on a mask and denying our true feelings
feels easier.

But God has no problem with us acknowledging how we feel
and telling Him what we fear. God is not a fair-weather friend who
will ask us to come back at a more convenient time. When we're
honest and bare our souls to God, He turns our mourning into hope.
In Psalm 43, David's lamentations lead him to explore his fears.
Ultimately, David concluded that he could put his hope only in
God. In the Psalms, David repeatedly expressed his fears, sorrows,
and regrets. He was also encouraged by God and praised Him for
strengthening and keeping him safe. In the same way, we can take
the time to express the deepest concerns of our soul to God.

ANXIETY RELIEF EXERCISE

Expressive Journaling (page 187). This exercise will help you express
what you've been thinking and feeling to God without holding anything back.

PRAYERS

Have you been hiding your true feelings from God? Ask God to help you be more honest with Him.

Are you willing to bare your soul to Him so He can carry your burdens and be the source of your hope? Take some time this week to tell Him what has been in your heart.

Day 1

_____

_____

_____

_____

_____

Day 2

_____

_____

_____

_____

_____

Day 3

_____

_____

_____

_____

_____

Day 4

_____

_____

_____

_____

_____

Day 5

_____

_____

_____

_____

_____

Day 6

_____

_____

_____

_____

_____

Day 7

_____

_____

_____

_____

_____

Week 3

BE STRONG AND COURAGEOUS

"Have not I commanded thee? Be strong and of a good courage; be not afraid, neither be thou dismayed: for the LORD thy God is with thee whithersoever thou goest."

JOSHUA 1:9

Do you feel that the cards you've been dealt have been difficult to handle? Anxious feelings often arise when it's difficult to predict the outcome of certain circumstances. God usually won't tell us *how* He will help us through a situation, but He promises that He is with us.

After the Israelites had been wandering in the wilderness for forty years, Joshua was tasked with leading them to the Promised Land of Canaan. The battles they would face to claim their land would not be easy, but Joshua knew that he could trust God to keep His promise of victory to His people. Joshua didn't know exactly how God would help him in all the battles, but God assured Joshua that he would not be alone.

When we remember this promise, we gain the courage to take small steps forward instead of running away from our battles. This doesn't mean we won't feel any anxiety when we move toward our next battle, but we can find comfort knowing that God is behind us. He will help us walk in faith during challenging times.

ANXIETY RELIEF EXERCISE

Action Planning (page 209). This exercise will help you act in faith and courage on things that God has been calling you to do.

PRAYERS

As you go through your week, review Joshua 1:9 as a reminder that God is with you even when you don't know how things will turn out.

How does being assured of God's presence shift your perspective?

What does it look like knowing God is with you during every battle you face?

Day 1

_____

_____

_____

_____

_____

Day 2

_____

_____

_____

_____

_____

Day 3

_____

_____

_____

_____

_____

Day 4

_____

_____

_____

_____

_____

Day 5

_____

_____

_____

_____

_____

Day 6

_____

_____

_____

_____

_____

Day 7

_____

_____

_____

_____

_____

Week 4

EXPLORE THE ROOT, NOT ONLY THE FRUIT

*"Abide in me, and I in you. As the branch cannot bear fruit of itself,
except it abide in the vine; no more can ye, except ye abide in me."*

JOHN 15:4

At times, I've experienced anxiety due to a looming deadline, but my anxiety actually stemmed from my fear of failure. When we struggle with anxiety, we may focus on managing the symptoms without exploring the root. And the root holds clues to how we can respond on a deeper level.

Checking our motives is one way to know if we are responding to our anxiety in a healthy way, and not just to symptoms. Sometimes, anxiety forces us into "fix-it" mode, which can induce more anxiety, overthinking, and ruminating if "fixing" remains our focus. If we surrender our worries to God, we can find peace in knowing that He will help us.

If we want clarity and wisdom, we must abide in God. The Holy Spirit can help reveal the seeds of anxiety in our lives so we can work to find freedom from it. This process will take time, consistent prayer, study of Scripture, patience, humility, and a willingness to hear from Him and receive wise counsel.

When we abide in God, we will bear the fruit of the Spirit, which includes love, joy, peace, patience, kindness, goodness, faithfulness, gentleness, and self-control (Galatians 5:22–23)—all traits that help us overcome anxiety.

ANXIETY RELIEF EXERCISE

Faulty Thinking Traps (page 191). Examine belief patterns that are likely to contribute to anxious thoughts.

PRAYERS

Where in your life have you focused on managing the fruit of anxiety over identifying the source? Ask God to help you identify how to begin uncovering the root of your anxiety.

Day 1

_____

_____

_____

_____

_____

Day 2

_____

_____

_____

_____

_____

Day 3

_____

_____

_____

_____

_____

Day 4

Day 5

Day 6

Day 7

Week 5
AVOID COUNTERFEIT COMFORTS

*"Come unto me, all ye that labour and are heavy laden, and
I will give you rest. Take my yoke upon you, and learn of me;
for I am meek and lowly in heart: and ye shall find rest unto
your souls. For my yoke is easy, and my burden is light."*

MATTHEW 11:28–30

When we feel anxious, it's easier to turn to anything but God, such
as excessive eating, online shopping, and mindless social media
consumption. While these things get our minds off our anxious
thoughts, they only relieve our anxiety temporarily.

Instead of turning to counterfeit comforts, we can turn to God
for true comfort. Jesus promises that when we come to Him, we will
receive rest for our souls. When we accept Him as our Savior, we
are yoked, or attached, to Him. When we take His yoke, He lightens
our burden and gives us the strength to carry our load. We do not
need to strive on our own. No matter how tired or weighed down
we are, He promises us rest and peace.

ANXIETY RELIEF EXERCISE

Replace Negative Habits (page 196). Our unhealthy habits often
signal a counterfeit comfort. One of the best ways to kick a negative
habit is to replace it with a helpful habit that you also enjoy. This is
known as the **Replacement Principle.** This week's exercise will help
you identify your triggers so you can replace your ineffective habits
with more fulfilling ones.

PRAYERS

What counterfeit comforts have you been turning to?

Talk to God about the ways you can turn to Him for comfort when you feel anxious.

Day 1

_____

_____

_____

_____

_____

Day 2

_____

_____

_____

_____

Day 3

_____

_____

_____

_____

_____

Day 4

_____

_____

_____

_____

_____

Day 5

_____

_____

_____

_____

_____

Day 6

_____

_____

_____

_____

Day 7

_____

_____

_____

_____

Week 6

THE ILLUSION OF CONTROL

"Therefore I say unto you, Take no thought for your life, what ye shall eat, or what ye shall drink; nor yet for your body, what ye shall put on. Is not the life more than meat, and the body than raiment? Behold the fowls of the air: for they sow not, neither do they reap, nor gather into barns; yet your heavenly Father feedeth them. Are ye not much better than they? Which of you by taking thought can add one cubit unto his stature?"

MATTHEW 6:25–27

The fear of not knowing or not having control of what will happen in the future is a common source of anxiety. We worry about all the things that could go wrong and attempt to alleviate this fear by predicting the future and preventing bad things from happening. We take matters into our own hands and rehearse tragic outcomes to prepare for the worst.

Jesus commands us to focus on seeking God's kingdom rather than worrying about the next day (Matthew 6:33), which means being willing to obey God and serve Him, rather than worrying about how our needs will be met. If God feeds the birds and clothes the lilies, we can trust Him to feed and clothe us. Our job is not to rely on our own ability to drive certain outcomes. We can trust that God will guide us and provide us with what we need.

ANXIETY RELIEF EXERCISE

Circle of Control (page 180). Use this exercise to practice distinguishing between what is in your realm of responsibility and what isn't. Learn to submit what isn't in your realm of responsibility to God's control and focus on what you can control through God's reveal.

PRAYERS

When has your anxiety led you to overthink about everything that could go wrong? How does overthinking impact your life?

The next time you are tempted to forecast and control the future, what can you do instead?

Day 1

_____

_____

_____

_____

_____

Day 2

_____

_____

_____

_____

_____

Day 3

_____

_____

_____

_____

_____

Day 4

Day 5

Day 6

Day 7

Week 7

YOUR VALUE IS NOT IN QUESTION

"Are not two sparrows sold for a farthing? and one of them shall not fall on the ground without your Father. But the very hairs of your head are all numbered. Fear ye not therefore, ye are of more value than many sparrows."

MATTHEW 10:29–31

In today's culture of hustling and overachieving, it's easy to get caught up in a performance-driven mindset. The world teaches us that we need to work hard to earn our place in our career. We measure our value and even tie our salvation to how well we perform at work. This kind of constant assessment makes us feel unworthy, puts us under a lot of pressure, and feeds into our anxiety.

However, as daughters of God, we inherit our position as a joint heir with Christ (Romans 8:17)—meaning we have a deep intimacy with God that is made possible through Jesus! This is not a position that is earned or deserved. It is given to us freely. God also qualifies us to perform the responsibilities assigned to our role. Therefore, we do not need to rely on our own strength; we need only to depend on His strength to do the work He requires of us. Remember, He knows everything about you, even something trivial, like the number of hairs on your head (Matthew 10:30). His love and grace are not earned, but freely given to each one of His children (Ephesians 2:8–9). When we understand this, we can experience immense gratitude and unburden ourselves from the pressure to perform!

ANXIETY RELIEF EXERCISE

Identity-Based Scripture Declarations (page 178). Remind yourself of your true value in Christ, which is based on your identity as God's daughter. When we can internalize our true worth as His daughters, we are less likely to place our value on external factors, like our career and how well we perform at work.

PRAYERS

In what ways have you tried to define your worth or status solely through things like work and career?

Knowing your value is not measured by things like work performance, how does this affect your daily interactions, work, and relationships?

Day 1

_____

_____

_____

_____

_____

Day 2

_____

_____

_____

_____

_____

Day 3

_____

_____

_____

_____

_____

Day 4

_____

_____

_____

_____

_____

Day 5

_____

_____

_____

_____

_____

Day 6

_____

_____

_____

_____

_____

Day 7

_____

_____

_____

_____

_____

THE BATTLE IN OUR MIND

"For God hath not given us the spirit of fear; but of power, and of love, and of a sound mind."

2 TIMOTHY 1:7

We are targeted by an enemy who tries to block us from living out God's purposes for us. Satan tempted Eve by twisting her thoughts about God and getting her to question God's Word (Genesis 3). Even now, Satan uses the same tactics and lies to make us question God's goodness and who we are. In doing so, Satan wishes to instill in us fear, anxiety, and distrust.

We can overcome this spiritual battle with the tools and weapons God provides for us. Pick up God's Word as a sword and use it to resist Satan, the same way Jesus did when He was tempted by the enemy in the wilderness (Matthew 4). When God's truth becomes a part of us, we can experience spiritual victories over our thought battles.

ANXIETY RELIEF EXERCISE

Battle Verses (page 203). This week's exercise will equip you with Bible verses to help you to overcome spiritual battles in your mind.

PRAYERS

In what ways have you relied on your own strength to fight spiritual battles?

What will you do differently the next time you experience a battle in your mind?

Day 1

_____

_____

_____

_____

_____

Day 2

_____

_____

_____

_____

Day 3

_____

_____

_____

_____

Day 4

_____

_____

_____

_____

_____

Day 5

_____

_____

_____

_____

_____

Day 6

_____

_____

_____

_____

_____

Day 7

_____

_____

_____

_____

_____

Week 9

LISTEN FOR HIS VOICE

"But Jesus said, Suffer little children, and forbid them not, to come unto me: for of such is the kingdom of heaven."

MATTHEW 19:14

Children are fascinating in their natural element. They can be so engrossed in whatever is captivating their attention. God wants us to be fully present like children so that we can connect deeply with Him and stand in awe as we experience His will done on Earth.

As adults, sometimes we respond to our anxiety by using distractions. There have been many times when I've used social media to escape because it was easier than facing the truth. When we distract ourselves, we end up blocking God out of our daily lives. But if we are willing to be present and attuned to His voice, He can lead us in our daily life.

ANXIETY RELIEF EXERCISE

Intentional Attention (page 211). This week's exercise will help you notice where your attention tends to focus and practice being in the present with God.

PRAYERS

When do you escape the present? Take some time this week to observe any instances of when you avoid being present. What might you miss out on by not being present?

Ask God to help you be more childlike so you can be more present and connected to Him.

Day 1

_____

_____

_____

_____

_____

Day 2

_____

_____

_____

_____

_____

Day 3

_____

_____

_____

_____

_____

Day 4

Day 5

Day 6

Day 7

Week 10

GOD IS OUR REFUGE

*"God is our refuge and strength, a very present help in trouble.
Therefore will not we fear, though the earth be removed, and
though the mountains be carried into the midst of the sea."*

PSALM 46:1–2

Not all anxiety is bad. Biologically, anxiety is designed to alert us to potential danger. When our brain detects a threat to our surroundings, our body responds in a way that enables us to fight or flee to safety. However, if we habitually detect a threat when there isn't any real danger, anxiety can become debilitating. One way to alleviate anxiety is by taking slow, deep breaths and reminding ourselves of God's presence and that we are indeed safe with Him. Then we can pay attention to what we may need in the moment. When we remember that God is a place of safety for us, we can run to Him as our refuge.

ANXIETY RELIEF EXERCISE

Hearing from God through Scripture (page 224). In this week's exercise, you will reflect on verses from God's Word that speak to your heart and give comfort when you need to turn to God as a refuge.

PRAYERS

Thank God for being a safe stronghold, protector, and defender. Meditate on these attributes of God.

What are some activities that help you feel safe and calm?

Day 1

_____

_____

_____

_____

_____

Day 2

_____

_____

_____

_____

_____

Day 3

_____

_____

_____

_____

_____

Day 4

_____
_____
_____
_____
_____

Day 5

_____
_____
_____
_____
_____

Day 6

_____
_____
_____
_____

Day 7

_____
_____
_____
_____
_____

Week 11

GOD IS WORKING IN YOU

"For it is God which worketh in you both to will
and to do of his good pleasure."

PHILIPPIANS 2:13

As Christians, we can easily get frustrated when old habits rear their ugly heads and remind us that we're not where we want to be in our walk with God. It can be discouraging when old habits seem impossible to kick.

The truth is, we are all works in progress and struggle in different ways. God does not expect you to purify your own heart. He will be with you each step of the way.

Instead of looking at ourselves and all the ways we fall short, we can focus on what God can do through His power. The power of God is working in you even when it doesn't feel like anything is happening. Change does not always happen as quickly as we'd like, but God is working in us. He is working to transform you from the inside to not only bring you closer to His will, but to expand your desire to live out what He has intended for you.

ANXIETY RELIEF EXERCISE

Answered Prayers and Praise Reports (page 220). In this week's exercise, you will reflect on what God has provided for you as a reminder of how much He has helped you.

PRAYERS

How does it feel to know that God is working in you to do what pleases Him? How does it feel to know that God is even fueling your desire to please Him?

Where has God been working in your life?

Day 1

_____

_____

_____

_____

_____

Day 2

_____

_____

_____

_____

_____

Day 3

_____

_____

_____

_____

_____

Day 4

_____

_____

_____

_____

_____

Day 5

_____

_____

_____

_____

_____

Day 6

_____

_____

_____

_____

_____

Day 7

_____

_____

_____

_____

_____

Week 12

GOD WILL GIVE YOU PEACE

"Be careful for nothing; but in every thing by prayer and supplication with thanksgiving let your requests be made known unto God. And the peace of God, which passeth all understanding, shall keep your hearts and minds through Christ Jesus."

PHILIPPIANS 4:6–7

We might think of peace as the result of the best circumstances, like financial stability, a clean bill of health, or perfect harmony in all our relationships. But God's peace is supernatural and isn't easily explained. It's peace even when the house is a mess, we haven't figured everything out, and our problems are unresolved. When we express our needs to Him, He listens and grants us peace, even in times of uncertainty and waiting. We can give all our cares and worries to God and rely on His peace to guard our hearts and minds, even in the middle of chaos.

ANXIETY RELIEF EXERCISE

Giving God Your Worries and Fears (page 207). This week's exercise will help you unload your cares to God so you can experience His peace.

PRAYERS

Have you asked God for what you need? Share the ways you are lacking peace with God.

In what ways has God's peace comforted you?

Day 1

_____

_____

_____

_____

_____

Day 2

_____

_____

_____

_____

_____

Day 3

_____

_____

_____

_____

_____

Day 4

Day 5

Day 6

Day 7

Week 13

GOD'S TRANSFORMATIVE POWER

*"And be not conformed to this world: but be ye transformed
by the renewing of your mind, that ye may prove what is
that good, and acceptable, and perfect, will of God."*

ROMANS 12:2

We might try to fix ourselves by modifying our outward behavior, but the changes we make will not sustain if our mind is not renewed. When we allow God to lead us, He continually transforms our heart and mind. Only He can help us change the thoughts that contribute to our anxiety. When we experience a change within, our actions will flow from the inside out and naturally reflect this change.

This process can take time, but we can trust that the Creator of our minds is transforming us even when we don't sense anything happening.

ANXIETY RELIEF EXERCISE

Replace Lies and Meditate on Truths (page 194). In this week's exercise, you will use Scriptures in God's Word to replace any faulty thinking traps that you have fallen into and immerse yourself in the truth of God's Word.

PRAYERS

Ask God to align your heart with Him and to move away from conforming to the world's ways.

In what ways do you want to be more aligned with the mind of Christ?

Day 1

_____

_____

_____

_____

_____

Day 2

_____

_____

_____

_____

_____

Day 3

_____

_____

_____

_____

_____

Day 4

_____

_____

_____

_____

_____

Day 5

_____

_____

_____

_____

_____

Day 6

_____

_____

_____

_____

_____

Day 7

_____

_____

_____

_____

_____

Week 14

GOD'S POWER MANIFESTED IN AFFLICTION

*"And his disciples asked him, saying, Master, who did sin, this
man, or his parents, that he was born blind? Jesus answered,
Neither hath this man sinned, nor his parents: but that the
works of God should be made manifest in him."*

JOHN 9:2–3

When Jesus and His disciples encountered a man who was born
blind, His disciples assumed that sin was the reason for the man's
blindness. They were so hung up on why the man was born blind
that they missed seeing how God was going to use the man's healing to reveal His power and glory.

In a similar way, we may assume that all our anxiety is from our
sin. We focus on the ways we fall short and believe that we're hope-
less. Sometimes there is no clear reason why we are experiencing
anxiety, but getting hung up on *why* certain things are happening
in our life can be a trap. Our troubles are an opportunity for God to
reveal His power, redirect us, and remind us that we are not meant
to fight these battles alone. Take comfort in knowing that God can
use our battles to demonstrate His power and free us from despair.

ANXIETY RELIEF EXERCISE

Seeing the Good (page 223). For this week's exercise, you will reflect
on the ways you've experienced good even in hard times.

PRAYERS

What important reminders or insights did you gain from this week's Scripture?

When have you experienced God's power amidst your anxiety?

Day 1

_____

_____

_____

_____

Day 2

_____

_____

_____

_____

Day 3

_____

_____

_____

_____

Day 4

_____

_____

_____

_____

_____

Day 5

_____

_____

_____

_____

_____

Day 6

_____

_____

_____

_____

_____

Day 7

_____

_____

_____

_____

_____

Week 15

GOD IS ALWAYS IN CONTROL

"I have planted, Apollos watered; but God gave the increase.
So then neither is he that planteth any thing, neither he
that watereth; but God that giveth the increase."

1 CORINTHIANS 3:6–7

Have you ever been so worried about the outcome of something that you ended up sabotaging yourself? When we experience uncertainty, it's easy to worry about where things can go wrong. Instead, we can commit our actions to God's will because He orchestrates everything in His perfect way.

We are responsible for our actions, our attitudes, and our own behavior. We are not responsible for changing other people or making sure that everything goes perfectly. We can trust that the ultimate outcome is in God's hands.

We may need to repent for the ways we've tried to play God. We can ask God to help us discern what is our responsibility and what isn't. It's possible that we're holding on too tightly to our own expectations when He's just asking for our willingness to obey Him.

ANXIETY RELIEF EXERCISE

Process Goals (page 182). In this week's exercise, you will set some goals to help you focus on the process of your journey and determine what is in your realm of responsibility, rather than fixating on a specific outcome.

PRAYERS

What areas in your life do you most want to submit to God? What areas in your life do you want to stop controlling? What areas in your life are preventing you from being closer to Him, His grace, and His power?

In your prayer time this week, ask God to reveal what is your responsibility and what isn't.

Day 1

_____

_____

_____

_____

_____

Day 2

_____

_____

_____

_____

_____

Day 3

_____

_____

_____

_____

_____

Day 4

_____

Day 5

_____

Day 6

_____

Day 7

_____

Week 16

OUR SECURITY IS IN CHRIST, NOT IN THIS WORLD

"These things I have spoken unto you, that in me ye might have peace. In the world ye shall have tribulation: but be of good cheer; I have overcome the world."

JOHN 16:33

At times, our lives feel like perpetual chaos, like we'll never catch a break. The Bible tells us that tribulations are inevitable, but Jesus overcame the trials in this world, and He guides us through our trials as well.

Times of crisis often reveal what is truly important to us. When the rug is pulled out from under us, we see that we've been putting all our security in our money, status, career, social approval, and so forth. Nothing in this world can give us eternal satisfaction the way God's peace can. Ultimately, this world is not our home. When we are in a relationship with God, we can have His peace, even in difficult times. When our hopes disappoint us, we can rest knowing we have an eternal Comforter in Him.

ANXIETY RELIEF EXERCISE

Intentional Attention (page 211). This week's exercise is designed to help you refocus your attention on God rather than continually getting caught up with everything in the material world.

PRAYERS

In what ways have you put your security in the material world?
     Ask God to help you experience His peace during any difficult challenges you will face this week.

Day 1

_____

_____

_____

_____

_____

Day 2

_____

_____

_____

_____

_____

Day 3

_____

_____

_____

_____

_____

Day 4

Day 5

Day 6

Day 7

Week 17

ANXIETY AS AN IMPORTANT MESSENGER

"And I will bring the blind by a way that they knew not; I will lead them in paths that they have not known: I will make darkness light before them, and crooked things straight. These things will I do unto them, and not forsake them."

ISAIAH 42:16

God can use our anxiety to shine His light on things that need to be examined in our lives. For example, God has shown me that I was experiencing anxiety because I had failed to set necessary boundaries as a steward of my gifts and time. When we need God's deliverance, He casts light on what needs to change in our lives so He can redirect us toward healing.

Every emotion we experience can act as an important messenger. When we habitually ignore our needs, our anxiety can eventually increase in intensity, making it more difficult to manage. Anxiety can be a signal that something requires our attention. God may be asking us to let go of certain wounds and ways of coping that don't add value to our lives other than prolonged stress and anxiety. When we're able to let these things go, we can begin healing and allow God to help us become more like Jesus. Like a parent coaxing a child who does not want to let go of a broken toy, God can't help us if we won't give our wounds to Him for healing.

ANXIETY RELIEF EXERCISE

Acknowledging Your Emotions (page 198). This week's exercise is designed to help you practice observing, identifying, and acknowledging your emotions so the Holy Spirit can help you manage and set them in their proper place.

PRAYERS

Ask God to show you what burdens, unresolved wounds, or thinking patterns need work in your life. Reflect and bring your thoughts to Him.

Day 1

_____

_____

_____

_____

Day 2

_____

_____

_____

_____

Day 3

_____

_____

_____

_____

Day 4

_____

_____

_____

_____

_____

Day 5

_____

_____

_____

_____

_____

Day 6

_____

_____

_____

_____

_____

Day 7

_____

_____

_____

_____

_____

GOD EMPOWERS US TO ENDURE

"There hath no temptation taken you but such as is common to man: but God is faithful, who will not suffer you to be tempted above that ye are able; but will with the temptation also make a way to escape, that ye may be able to bear it."

1 CORINTHIANS 10:13

When I became a new Christian, I thought I would be in a constant state of elation and that most of my problems would go away. I was in for a rude awakening. God never promised a life free of pain or temptation. But no matter what we go through, He promises to help us endure.

When we experience anxiety, we have a choice: rely on God, run away, or take control of things and try to take on the role of God.

While experiencing anxiety does not automatically mean we are sinning, how we choose to respond to it matters. When we use anxiety as an excuse to act sinfully, we put anxiety at a higher place than God and we allow it to have more power than God. Rather than trusting in just ourselves, we can turn to God. He will always help us respond to our anxiety in a way that refines us and keeps us from hurting ourselves and others.

ANXIETY RELIEF EXERCISE

Replace Negative Habits (page 196). In this week's exercise, you will identify and replace certain unhelpful habits that may be triggered by certain uncomfortable feelings, like anxiety.

PRAYERS

When you experience anxiety, do you trust God to help you endure difficult situations?

Ask God for wisdom when navigating the temptation to give in to your anxiety.

Ask God for strength to rely on Him rather than taking control yourself.

Day 1

_____

_____

_____

_____

_____

Day 2

_____

_____

_____

_____

_____

Day 3

_____

_____

_____

_____

_____

Day 4

_____

_____

_____

_____

_____

Day 5

_____

_____

_____

_____

_____

Day 6

_____

_____

_____

_____

_____

Day 7

_____

_____

_____

_____

_____

JESUS KNOWS EXACTLY HOW WE FEEL

"For we have not an high priest which cannot be touched with the feeling of our infirmities; but was in all points tempted like as we are, yet without sin. Let us therefore come boldly unto the throne of grace, that we may obtain mercy, and find grace to help in time of need."

HEBREWS 4:15–16

Jesus feels the same difficult emotions we experience—deep anguish, sorrow, and anger because of sin. We do not need to demonize our emotions, because our Lord understands the complexity of how we feel. He understands our feelings better than we understand our own feelings.

There are times that our infirmities or weaknesses overwhelm us, and it's easy to doubt that God can transform the parts of us that need healing. So we pretend they don't exist or try to push them away. It is important to remember during these times that Jesus does not condemn us. Instead, Jesus asks us to boldly come to His throne, where grace and mercy reign. Who better to ask for help than someone who has already felt everything we've felt, currently feel, and are going to feel? Will you boldly come and ask for help today?

ANXIETY RELIEF EXERCISE

Acknowledging Your Emotions (page 198). In this week's exercise, practice identifying what you feel, and be honest with God without automatically condemning yourself for your struggles.

PRAYERS

How does it feel to know Jesus experienced similar emotions as you? How does that change how you view your own emotions?

Day 1

Day 2

Day 3

Day 4

Day 5

Day 6

Day 7

LOOK AT JESUS

"And he said, Come. And when Peter was come down out of the ship, he walked on the water, to go to Jesus. But when he saw the wind boisterous, he was afraid; and beginning to sink, he cried, saying, Lord, save me. And immediately Jesus stretched forth his hand, and caught him, and said unto him, O thou of little faith, wherefore didst thou doubt?"

MATTHEW 14:29–31

When Peter saw Jesus on the water, he stepped out of the boat to walk toward Him. As long as Peter kept his eyes on Jesus, he was able to remain on top of the water. But as soon as he turned to the waves around him, he began to sink. The lesson? When we focus on our circumstances, we can get completely engulfed.

Sometimes I magnify an issue in my head so much that I can't bring myself to clearly see Jesus. My worries create a fog that impairs my vision, and Jesus becomes hidden. Instead of calling out to Jesus, I sink into despair. When I do remember to call on Jesus, His presence becomes apparent. Only then can I face the storm, feeling reassured knowing that no matter what is ahead of me, I will be okay as long as I focus on Him.

ANXIETY RELIEF EXERCISE

Giving God Your Worries and Fears (page 207). In this week's exercise, take some time to cast your fears and worries onto Jesus so that He can carry all your burdens.

PRAYERS

In what ways have you been looking at your problems more than looking at Jesus?

What does Peter's experience of walking on water show you about how you should respond to current challenges?

Day 1

_____

_____

_____

_____

_____

Day 2

_____

_____

_____

_____

_____

Day 3

_____

_____

_____

_____

_____

Day 4

_____

_____

_____

_____

_____

Day 5

_____

_____

_____

_____

_____

Day 6

_____

_____

_____

_____

_____

Day 7

_____

_____

_____

_____

_____

Week 21

KEEP YOUR EYES ON ETERNITY

"Set your affection on things above, not on things on the earth."

COLOSSIANS 3:2

It's easy to get wrapped up in our endless to-do lists and grow puffed up at what we've achieved.

When our energy, hopes, and expectations are directed toward earthly accomplishments, we easily become disillusioned over time. We feel deeply disappointed. A relationship ends or our career trajectory doesn't look the way we had hoped.

But when our perspective is set on heaven, our earthly cares appear much smaller.

Setting our mind on eternity is an active choice. When we question, "Will this matter a year from now? How about five years? How about in eternity?" we can see what we really need to focus on. Looking through the lens of eternity can help us gain a wider vision and understanding of God's purpose, especially in disappointing situations when we feel entitled to certain outcomes.

ANXIETY RELIEF EXERCISE

Intentional Attention (page 211). In this week's exercise, you will practice focusing your attention on God's Word and reminding yourself of what's truly important every day.

PRAYERS

What would you like to remind yourself of the next time you need to refocus your mind to an eternal perspective?

What are some things that you're looking forward to about heaven?

Day 1

_____

_____

_____

_____

_____

Day 2

_____

_____

_____

_____

_____

Day 3

_____

_____

_____

_____

_____

Day 4

_____

_____

_____

_____

_____

Day 5

_____

_____

_____

_____

_____

Day 6

_____

_____

_____

_____

_____

Day 7

_____

_____

_____

_____

_____

Week 22
THE SWINGING PENDULUM

"Finally, brethren, whatsoever things are true, whatsoever things are honest, whatsoever things are just, whatsoever things are pure, whatsoever things are lovely, whatsoever things are of good report; if there be any virtue, and if there be any praise, think on these things."

PHILIPPIANS 4:8

Being reactive is very common when our anxiety is at its peak. We can swing from one side of a pendulum to another. If we've been hurt after letting someone in, it's natural to want to close ourselves off from everyone. We are likely to paint people or events with one broad brush and see them as either one hundred percent good or one hundred percent bad. When we get in this mode, we swing between episodes of idealizing and idolizing to demonizing and catastrophizing. When we're swinging on the pendulum, there is no room for nuance or flexibility to adapt to our circumstances.

The next time you find yourself veering to extreme thought patterns, take some time to pause and observe what is happening. Then take a moment to ask the Holy Spirit to reveal the truth and pray for the wisdom to respond appropriately.

Sometimes the best response is not to do anything at all. Instead of taking the path of least resistance and giving in to a knee-jerk reaction, we can ask the Holy Spirit to give us wisdom and discernment, moment by moment.

ANXIETY RELIEF EXERCISE

Faulty Thinking Traps (page 191). This week's exercise will help you identify any thinking patterns that are trapping you into an extreme black or white stance.

PRAYERS

Have you recognized any extreme thinking patterns in yourself?
Towards God?

Ask God to give you wisdom and discernment when you find
yourself in a heightened state of anxiety.

Day 1

_____
_____
_____
_____
_____

Day 2

_____
_____
_____
_____
_____

Day 3

_____
_____
_____
_____
_____

Day 4

_____

_____

_____

_____

Day 5

_____

_____

_____

_____

Day 6

_____

_____

_____

_____

Day 7

_____

_____

_____

_____

GOD'S SOVEREIGN WILL

"Thy kingdom come, Thy will be done in earth, as it is in heaven."

MATTHEW 6:10

One of my greatest fears is that I will fail God and make a mistake so big that even He can't fix it. When I'm consumed by this fear, I remember that no matter what, I cannot mess up God's will on Earth. It's a relief that I don't have that kind of power.

I also try to remember that what matters most is that I'm willing to submit my own will to His. I know there is nothing I can do apart from Him. When we are focused on allowing His will to be done, we release the need to control our destiny and future. We don't have to worry or feel anxious about messing up.

God promises that when we surrender our will to His, He will mold and shape our desire to reflect His. When He changes our heart in this way, He helps us align ourselves to His will.

ANXIETY RELIEF EXERCISE

Circle of Control (page 180). This week's exercise will remind you of what is in God's sovereign will and help build trust in Him to take care of what isn't in your control.

PRAYERS

What is your response to knowing that God's will is going to be fulfilled no matter what?

What areas of your life would you like to submit to His will?

Day 1

_____

_____

_____

_____

_____

Day 2

_____

_____

_____

_____

_____

Day 3

_____

_____

_____

_____

_____

Day 4

_____

_____

_____

_____

_____

Day 5

_____

_____

_____

_____

_____

Day 6

_____

_____

_____

_____

_____

Day 7

_____

_____

_____

_____

_____

Week 24

WE ARE SERVANTS OF GOD, NOT PEOPLE PLEASERS

"For do I now persuade men, or God? or do I seek to please men?
for if I yet pleased men, I should not be the servant of Christ."

GALATIANS 1:10

Many women are relational beings who thrive in a community. God has given women the gift to influence others without exerting control or aggression. This ability is a beautiful strength when used for God's kingdom. However, when we focus our energy on pleasing people more than pleasing God, we can fall into patterns of rescuing others and playing God in their lives or allowing people to play God in our lives. Letting God work in other people's hearts is much better than imposing our ideas onto them.

We tend to care about what people think of us, but God can alleviate our fears of rejection or abandonment. When we allow God to lead, we serve others with a pure heart instead of our desires to rescue or receive approval. With a pure heart, we can demonstrate a love that is transformational, not transactional.

ANXIETY RELIEF EXERCISE

Taking Off Your Masks (page 218). Use this week's exercise to start taking off different masks (including the people-pleaser mask) that you may be hiding behind so that you can live authentically and walk in your true identity in Christ.

PRAYERS

In what ways do you experience anxiety related to people pleasing?

Ask God to show you how you can serve others in a way that reflects your obedience to Him, rather than turning to people pleasing.

Day 1

_____

_____

_____

_____

_____

Day 2

_____

_____

_____

_____

_____

Day 3

_____

_____

_____

_____

_____

Day 4

Day 5

Day 6

Day 7

TAKING CARE OF OUR TEMPLE

"What? know ye not that your body is the temple of the Holy Ghost which is in you, which ye have of God, and ye are not your own?"

1 CORINTHIANS 6:19

We've all heard the term self-care, but I prefer the term "temple care." Temple care is about stewarding the physical body God has given to us. Not only is taking time to rest important, but it gives us space to pay attention to where we are investing our time and energy. This isn't to be mistaken with self-indulgence and self-idolatry. Passing on a dinner invite to take some time at home to rest or taking time off work to be with God could be exactly what you need.

Jesus took time to rest, take breaks from people, and to be alone with God. When we don't take time to be with God, our temple suffers. When we are continually meeting the demands of others and our environment, we can become accustomed to running on adrenaline and eventually burn out.

ANXIETY RELIEF EXERCISE

"Pick Me Up" List (page 205). This week's exercise will give you an opportunity to identify and engage in invigorating activities that will help reset your body, mind, and soul.

PRAYERS

What do you currently do to take care of your temple?

What are some habits you'd like to develop to continue taking care of your temple?

Ask God to help show you healthy ways of restoring your temple.

Day 1

_____

_____

_____

_____

_____

Day 2

_____

_____

_____

_____

_____

Day 3

_____

_____

_____

_____

_____

Day 4

Day 5

Day 6

Day 7

Week 26

GOD WILL NEVER CAST YOU OUT

*"All that the Father giveth me shall come to me; and him
that cometh to me I will in no wise cast out."*

JOHN 6:37

We may have experienced rejection or abandonment. As a result, relationships can be a trigger for our anxiety and fear of rejection, like when we show all our cards to others and are met with dismissiveness. When we've had many experiences like this, it's understandable to retreat from people.

Even through experiences of rejection, I take comfort in knowing that God will never abandon me or cast me out of His kingdom. People can be fickle, but God is not. He sees us exactly as we are, but His love remains the same. He is always there for us. He promises that He will never cast us away or abandon us.

ANXIETY RELIEF EXERCISE

Identity-Based Scripture Declarations (page 178). In this week's exercise, you will meditate on truths related to your true identity in Christ to remind you that God will never leave or abandon you.

PRAYERS

Whenever you feel alone, remind yourself of John 6:37. What does it mean to you that God will never cast out His children?

Day 1

_____

_____

_____

_____

_____

Day 2

_____

_____

_____

_____

Day 3

_____

_____

_____

_____

Day 4

_____

_____

_____

_____

_____

Day 5

_____

_____

_____

_____

_____

Day 6

_____

_____

_____

_____

_____

Day 7

_____

_____

_____

_____

_____

Week 27

GOD QUALIFIES THE CALLED

"And Moses said unto God, Who am I, that I should go unto Pharaoh, and that I should bring forth the children of Israel out of Egypt? And he said, Certainly I will be with thee; and this shall be a token unto thee, that I have sent thee: When thou hast brought forth the people out of Egypt, ye shall serve God upon this mountain."

EXODUS 3:11–12

After Harriet Tubman gained her freedom from slavery, she returned to the South over the course of ten years and helped many more slaves escape. She was nicknamed the "Moses" of her people, as an analogy to the way Moses led the Israelites out of captivity.

Like Tubman, our calling often involves something that burdens our heart. That is, God may put a burden on our heart so He can use us to lead and/or help others. When God called me to coaching, I questioned if He was mistaking me for someone else. I felt underqualified. God reminded me that many women were suffering from a lack of spiritual knowledge in their lives (Hosea 4:6), and I could use my own journey of overcoming anxiety to help others. I am still a work in progress but God reminds me that He helped me experience freedom in Christ. I can encourage other women to turn to Him too. I still feel underqualified at times, but He has never failed to come through when I've allowed Him to lead.

ANXIETY RELIEF EXERCISE

Process Goals (page 182). For this week's exercise, you will explore what you believe God has been calling you to do in this season. Set some goals to prioritize the responsibilities God has been calling you to fulfill.

PRAYERS

In what areas of your life have you felt unqualified? How did you respond?

What challenges has God been calling you to boldly face?

What fears or worries do you have about stepping into your calling? Take some time to share those fears with God. Ask Him to show you the ways in which you can rely on Him to equip you.

Day 1

Day 2

Day 3

Day 4

_____

_____

_____

_____

_____

Day 5

_____

_____

_____

_____

_____

Day 6

_____

_____

_____

_____

_____

Day 7

_____

_____

_____

_____

_____

Week 28

DIVINE APPOINTMENTS

*"Go, gather together all the Jews that are present in Shushan, and
fast ye for me, and neither eat nor drink three days, night or day: I
also and my maidens will fast likewise; and so will I go in unto the
king, which is not according to the law: and if I perish, I perish."*

ESTHER 4:16

The story of Esther is filled with unexpected turns of events. As an
orphaned Jew who was adopted by her cousin Mordecai, Esther
won a beauty contest to become the new queen of Persia. When
the king's adviser, Haman, plotted to have all Jews annihilated,
Mordecai begged Esther to confront the king even though she
could have received the death penalty for doing so. Esther asked
Mordecai to gather all the Jews to fast and pray with her and her
maidens for three days.

Esther's response shows us that she was not relying on herself,
but instead seeking God through prayer and fasting. God had put
her in the right time and place to set her up for a divine calling
to save the Jews from genocide. Willing to risk her life, she con-
fronted the king, which ultimately led her to save her people from
destruction.

God uses those who are humble and willing to depend on Him
to carry out His calling. When God calls us to take risks, we can trust
Him to orchestrate His divine plans.

ANXIETY RELIEF EXERCISE

Battle Prayers (page 201). In this week's exercise, you will have the
opportunity to prepare battle prayers like Esther when you encounter hardship and opposition.

PRAYERS

Take some time to read the book of Esther this week and reflect on her response to a divine calling. What does Esther's story demonstrate about navigating difficult situations?

Reflect on any situations you've been in that required risk or sacrifice. How did you respond? How do you want to respond in future challenging situations?

Day 1

Day 2

Day 3

Day 4

Day 5

Day 6

Day 7

Week 29

GOD CAN REDEEM ALL THINGS

"And we know that all things work together for good to them that love God, to them who are the called according to his purpose."

ROMANS 8:28

In past seasons of deep depression and anxiety, hearing that God could work my suffering for good felt like a platitude and even downright dismissive. I had a very hard time believing this could be true and had no idea how God could use my pain. But God has shown me day by day and moment by moment that He can be trusted. I wish I could say I trusted Him with everything in just one big leap of faith. Over time, I let Him in slowly and allowed Him to lead me in different areas of my life. Sometimes, I still need to be reminded to let Him lead me, but He has never once failed me.

I am reminded that God has worked my pain for good every time I support a woman who feels seen and who no longer feels like they are walking alone. Today, I can see that everything I've gone through has not been wasted. I've witnessed my past being redeemed for His glory, and it has equipped me to serve others. When I share with a client about a lesson I've learned the hard way, I often see their eyes light up with hope and excitement as they tell me how seen and understood they feel. In these moments, the joy of serving others greatly outweighs any of the suffering I've experienced in my past. I know I couldn't have felt this joy if I hadn't gone through everything that I had.

ANXIETY RELIEF EXERCISE

Seeing the Good (page 223). For this week's exercise, you will reflect on the good you have experienced and how God is redeeming your past despite your suffering through trying times.

PRAYERS

Take some time to meditate on what it means to you for God to work all things for your good. In what areas of your life would you like God to work out for your good?

Where in your life can you take baby steps to submit to God?

Day 1

_____

_____

_____

_____

_____

Day 2

_____

_____

_____

_____

_____

Day 3

_____

_____

_____

_____

_____

Day 4

Day 5

Day 6

Day 7

Week 30

WAIT ON THE LORD

"But they that wait upon the LORD shall renew their strength; they shall mount up with wings as eagles; they shall run, and not be weary; and they shall walk, and not faint."

ISAIAH 40:31

When we're in turmoil, doubts about God's goodness can creep into our minds. When we feel ignored by God, it's easy to get into "fix-it" mode and think we need to take control of a situation. But when I trust God to lead, I've found that I can persevere much longer than when I've devised my own ideas and plans.

If we take it upon ourselves to fix things with our own strength and from our narrow perspective, we will likely run out of steam, and our solution will be limited, compared to God's plans. God asks us to be patient as it takes time to bear fruit and see the result of the work He has been doing.

We are not guaranteed a trouble-free life, but God promises to give us the strength we need. In times of crisis, we are called to turn to God for His help and direction. Sometimes His instruction is for us to act, and other times He asks us to be still and allow Him to work.

ANXIETY RELIEF EXERCISE

Reality Testing (page 193). Sometimes when we experience turmoil, we feel compelled to take action immediately. In this week's exercise, you will pause, examine, and test your beliefs about a situation before going into "fix-it" mode.

PRAYERS

When you experience anxiety, what makes it difficult for you to wait on the Lord?

Think about past situations you've experienced that required waiting. What was the outcome of waiting and being still?

In what areas of your life can you make more room for God to lead?

Day 1

_____

_____

_____

_____

Day 2

_____

_____

_____

_____

Day 3

_____

_____

_____

_____

Day 4

_____

_____

_____

_____

Day 5

_____

_____

_____

_____

Day 6

_____

_____

_____

_____

Day 7

_____

_____

_____

_____

Week 31

EXPERIENCE TRUE JOY

"Thou wilt shew me the path of life: in thy presence is fulness of joy; at thy right hand there are pleasures for evermore."

PSALM 16:11

In past seasons of extreme hopelessness, I constantly worried about why my life had not turned out the way I thought it should. I feared that I'd never amount to anything, and the shame paralyzed and isolated me. During this time, God began to draw me to a deeper connection with Him. He asked me to spend more time with Him in prayer, be more honest with Him, and surrender all my cares to Him. I found contentment in Him over worldly desires like my career, my relationships, and my material possessions. If I hadn't experienced a season where I felt He was all I had, I don't know that I would've learned to depend on God. Instead of following a path that I was once sure would lead me to happiness, I trusted Him to direct my life and found true joy.

When we experience anxiety, it's hard to remember that our joy doesn't depend on our circumstances. Apart from God, we experience emotional highs that fade, but when we follow God, we can experience true joy.

ANXIETY RELIEF EXERCISE

Receiving God's Love and Compassion (page 216). The goal of this week's exercise is to help bring you into God's presence more regularly so that you can experience the fullness of His joy.

PRAYERS

In the past, what have you believed would bring you joy?

Recall the times when you've experienced joy from being in God's presence. How did it compare to other positive experiences or emotions you've felt?

How would you like to seek God's presence this week? What would you like to pray to Him as you seek His presence?

Day 1

Day 2

Day 3

Day 4

_____

_____

_____

_____

_____

Day 5

_____

_____

_____

_____

_____

Day 6

_____

_____

_____

_____

_____

Day 7

_____

_____

_____

_____

Week 32

GUARD YOUR HEART AND MIND

"For where your treasure is, there will your heart be also."

MATTHEW 6:21

When something appeals to our senses and is advertised as the key to our happiness—an advertisement or a movie, a burger you didn't know you wanted until you saw it on a billboard, or a pristine white kitchen you saw on Instagram—it's very easy to be enticed and fall into the trap of covetousness.

We must guard our minds and hearts because what we allow ourselves to consume can feed our anxiety and fear and ultimately turn us away from God. Over time, we stop being aware of which thoughts are ours and which thoughts have been programmed into our minds.

Guarding our hearts can look like limiting the time we spend watching the news, staying away from certain types of entertainment, and distancing ourselves from certain people. Instead, we can turn to God so He can reveal what is truth and give us the peace that comes with being close to Him.

ANXIETY RELIEF EXERCISE

Set Boundaries to Guard Your Mind and Heart (page 213). In this week's exercise, take some time to revisit the concept of boundaries and evaluate if there are any more boundaries that you need to guard your mind and heart.

PRAYERS

What external influences or habits introduce faulty thinking patterns into your mind?

What steps can you take to guard your heart and mind? Ask God to help you set boundaries so you can keep your eyes on God and His kingdom.

Day 1

_____

_____

_____

_____

Day 2

_____

_____

_____

_____

Day 3

_____

_____

_____

_____

Day 4

_____

_____

_____

_____

_____

Day 5

_____

_____

_____

_____

_____

Day 6

_____

_____

_____

_____

_____

Day 7

_____

_____

_____

_____

_____

Week 33

COLORING BEYOND THE LINES

"Woe unto you, scribes and Pharisees, hypocrites! for ye are like unto whited sepulchres, which indeed appear beautiful outward, but are within full of dead men's bones, and of all uncleanness."

MATTHEW 23:27

I am a recovering perfectionist. There's a voice in my head that tells me my work is subpar, at best. I've thought to myself, "If I just work a bit longer, maybe then I can perfect it." Or, "If I could just read at least three chapters of the Bible a day, then I could call myself a good Christian." Unfortunately, this kind of thinking has caused me a lot of anxiety and has made me procrastinate and sabotage many projects.

We can try to make everything look perfect, but as Jesus told the Pharisees, even if a person looks beautiful on the outside, their insides can be unclean. The Pharisees were so concerned with appearing religious through their own man-made rules, but on the inside, their hearts were not transformed.

While in prayer, I once experienced the Holy Spirit telling me He wanted me to get comfortable coloring outside the lines. I realized He was asking me to stop subscribing to my own ideas and formulas for achieving perfection and, instead, allow Him to lead me and transform my heart.

ANXIETY RELIEF EXERCISE

Reality Testing (page 193). In this week's exercise, you will examine your beliefs against the truth to identify whether any of them reflect "man-made" rules or perfectionism.

PRAYERS

What are some perfectionist ideas that you've subscribed to?

What might it look like for you to color outside the lines and allow God to lead you?

Are there any ways you believe God wants to transform your heart?

Day 1

_____

_____

_____

_____

_____

Day 2

_____

_____

_____

_____

_____

Day 3

_____

_____

_____

_____

_____

Day 4

_____

_____

_____

_____

_____

Day 5

_____

_____

_____

_____

_____

Day 6

_____

_____

_____

_____

_____

Day 7

_____

_____

_____

_____

GOD'S HEALING

"O LORD my God, I cried unto thee, and thou hast healed me."

PSALM 30:2

Oftentimes, our anxiety is rooted in past experiences. Something in the present reminds us of someone who hurt us, a past failure, or something we've lost.

In the past, I've interpreted rejection and failure as evidence that I was irreparably broken. In these times of despair, I've cried out to God for help. I came to Him with the broken pieces of my heart, and He started to heal me. He helped me see that I had taken on brokenness as a false identity. God showed me through His love that I was giving into lies about who I was. I started to see that I had a purpose and position in His kingdom.

Healing is a process and an ongoing journey. Now I know that God will never turn away from me, even in my brokenness. I can always count on His grace and know that He is able to transform my past pain into joy, wisdom, and peace.

ANXIETY RELIEF EXERCISE

Receiving God's Love and Compassion (page 216). For this week's exercise, you will reflect on the meaning of God's love and take some practical steps to help yourself receive it.

PRAYERS

What areas of your life can you ask God to heal today?
Are there any false identities about brokenness that you have taken on in your life?

Day 1

_____

_____

_____

_____

_____

Day 2

_____

_____

_____

_____

_____

Day 3

_____

_____

_____

_____

_____

Day 4

_____
_____
_____
_____
_____

Day 5

_____
_____
_____
_____
_____

Day 6

_____
_____
_____
_____
_____

Day 7

_____
_____
_____
_____
_____

Week 35

RECEIVE GOD'S GOODNESS

"Yea, they turned back and tempted God, and limited the
Holy One of Israel. They remembered not his hand, nor
the day when he delivered them from the enemy."

PSALM 78:41–42

When we come up against an obstacle and are distressed or discouraged, we can feel as though God has forgotten about us. If we've been disappointed by others in the past, it's easy to project that disappointment onto God and expect Him to fail us as well.

Also, we tend to easily forget the times when God was with us. When God freed the Israelites from Egypt, He provided them with manna, the food of angels, which literally fell from heaven! But on their journey to the Promised Land, they complained, fell into unbelief, built a golden calf to worship instead of God, and even thought it would have been better if they had remained in Egypt! They'd completely forgotten everything God had done and was doing for them.

When we look at our discouraging circumstances, instead of believing God will lead us to freedom, it's easy to turn back to our old ways. God knows we will fall away from faith at times because we are human, but our unbelief has more to do with the limitations we impose on God, never due to His limitations. This passage is a sober reminder that lacking faith limits what God can and will do in our lives.

ANXIETY RELIEF EXERCISE

Answered Prayers and Praise Reports (page 220). This week's exercise is designed to help you focus on the good that God has done in your life and help ground you in your faith.

PRAYERS

Reflect on some past times that God came through for you. What can you do to avoid falling into unbelief?

Day 1

_____

_____

_____

_____

_____

Day 2

_____

_____

_____

_____

Day 3

_____

_____

_____

_____

Day 4

_____

_____

_____

_____

_____

Day 5

_____

_____

_____

_____

_____

Day 6

_____

_____

_____

_____

_____

Day 7

_____

_____

_____

_____

_____

Week 36

OVERCOMING GENERATIONAL BELIEFS

*"Not that we are sufficient of ourselves to think any thing
as of ourselves; but our sufficiency is of God."*

2 CORINTHIANS 3:5

As a daughter of immigrants, I felt immense pressure to succeed. I later realized that I had adopted some beliefs from previous generations, such as my grandparents who lived through the Korean War. It made sense that people who had to do everything they could to survive the war would believe that achieving financial stability was the key to a happy life.

I also learned that asking for help or expressing emotions meant I was weak. I didn't know how to rely on anyone, including God. In a survival mindset, I let fear control me; I thought I had to do everything by myself. Instead of moving forward in boldness and courage, I held myself back from taking risks. I avoided situations where I might fail because I believed I wasn't worthy of love if I didn't perform.

Over time, I realized God loves me unconditionally, regardless of what I do. I no longer play the role of Supergirl because I am not on my own. I don't need to live in fear because I know God will help me complete everything He wants me to accomplish.

ANXIETY RELIEF EXERCISE

Faulty Thinking Traps (page 191). This week's exercise will help you identify any thinking patterns you hold that are rooted in generational beliefs.

PRAYERS

Think about what you heard growing up about topics such as money, relationships, marriage, and career success. What are some generational patterns, ideas, or beliefs that have shaped your world view? How have they impacted you negatively or positively and do any need to be reframed?

   What are some burdens you've been holding onto that you can ask God to help carry?

Day 1

_____

_____

_____

_____

_____

Day 2

_____

_____

_____

_____

Day 3

_____

_____

_____

_____

Day 4

_____

_____

_____

_____

_____

Day 5

_____

_____

_____

_____

_____

Day 6

_____

_____

_____

_____

_____

Day 7

_____

_____

_____

_____

_____

Week 37
CALL ON HIM

"If a son shall ask bread of any of you that is a father, will he give him a stone? or if he ask a fish, will he for a fish give him a serpent?"

LUKE 11:11

Have you ever been in a situation where you've been panicking and worrying about something then suddenly remember you haven't asked God for what you need? Time and time again, I've experienced my anxiety subside after a panicked prayer to God. There are times when I am given peace about the situation, and there are times God directs me what to do.

Sometimes we forget God is a Father who loves His daughters, and we can call on Him at any time. Sometimes it feels like we're bothering Him or that we've asked for too much. Sometimes we're afraid that we'll ask but won't receive, or worse: receive something we don't want.

God asks us to come humbly to Him to receive His love, blessings, forgiveness, mercy, and grace. Being able to receive is an important part of our relationship with God. Sometimes we might have a hard time receiving, especially if your experiences have conditioned you to associate receiving with strings attached. But God enjoys blessing us abundantly and knows exactly what we need and want. Whatever He gives to us, He will give like a loving Father who gives good gifts to His daughters.

ANXIETY RELIEF EXERCISE

Meditate on God's Nature as Our Father (page 221). Sometimes we forget to ask God for what we want and need. This week's exercise will remind you that God is a loving Father who enjoys blessing us as His daughters.

PRAYERS

What has stopped you in the past from asking for what you need from God?

What steps can you take to pray with confidence in the future?

Day 1

_____

_____

_____

_____

_____

Day 2

_____

_____

_____

_____

_____

Day 3

_____

_____

_____

_____

_____

Day 4

_____
_____
_____
_____
_____

Day 5

_____
_____
_____
_____
_____

Day 6

_____
_____
_____
_____
_____

Day 7

_____
_____
_____
_____

Week 38

RECOGNIZING GOD'S VOICE

*"Even the Spirit of truth; whom the world cannot receive,
because it seeth him not, neither knoweth him: but ye know
him; for he dwelleth with you, and shall be in you."*

JOHN 14:17

We are bombarded with countless messages from the media, society, culture, and our families. Some of these messages become a part of our inner dialogue and play in our minds on repeat. If left unchecked, these messages can induce anxiety and fear.

Sometimes these voices even try to imitate the voice of the Holy Spirit. Many of my clients have told me that they've seen God as a punitive angry critic, but when we dig deeper into these thoughts, it's often revealed that their mindset toward God was based on a hypercritical parent or other family member. The truth is that even if our mother and father forsake us, God will never abandon His daughters (Psalm 27:10).

We can gain a true understanding of God's voice by reading about His true character in the Bible. When the Holy Spirit points to something that needs our attention, He won't leave us hanging. He will also comfort, lead, and equip us.

ANXIETY RELIEF EXERCISE

Replace Lies and Meditate on Truths (page 194). This week's exercise is designed to help you replace any faulty thinking traps or lies with the truth of God's Word so you can learn to better recognize God's voice.

PRAYERS

Take some time this week to observe the different voices or messages that show up in your inner dialogue. You can give them
names or labels if you find it helpful to recognize and identify them.

If you notice some patterns in your inner dialogue, try to discern
whether you are experiencing God's voice by testing it against what
the Bible says about God's character.

Day 1

Day 2

Day 3

Day 4

Day 5

Day 6

Day 7

Week 39

HIS SUFFICIENT GRACE

"And he said unto me, My grace is sufficient for thee: for my strength is made perfect in weakness. Most gladly therefore will I rather glory in my infirmities, that the power of Christ may rest upon me. Therefore I take pleasure in infirmities, in reproaches, in necessities, in persecutions, in distresses for Christ's sake: for when I am weak, then am I strong."

2 CORINTHIANS 12:9–10

Sometimes our anxiety can stem from being fixated on our physical condition and circumstances. While we may struggle with a physical weakness, God is more concerned about the spiritual condition of our heart.

Paul experienced a "thorn" in the flesh and asked God to take it away three times. Instead of removing it, however, God explained to Paul that His grace was sufficient in spite of the thorn. When we experience weakness, we feel broken and distraught, but God tells us that our weakness can be an opportunity to experience His power.

When we experience anxiety, we are reminded of our human weakness. Sometimes we try to pray to God to ask Him to remove it. We even try to hide it or rely on ourselves to fix it, but God wants us to bring our weaknesses to Him and rely on His sufficient grace. No matter what life throws at us, His grace can empower us to endure it. We can even experience joy when we see that our weaknesses are an opportunity for Him to demonstrate His power.

ANXIETY RELIEF EXERCISE

Seeing the Good (page 223). This week's exercise will remind you of God's sufficient grace even in the midst of trials.

PRAYERS

What anxieties do you need to bring to God today?

What does it mean to be strong in your weakness?

Take some time to reflect on situations where you experienced discomfort, but also spiritual growth.

Day 1

_____

_____

_____

_____

_____

Day 2

_____

_____

_____

_____

Day 3

_____

_____

_____

_____

Day 4

_____

_____

_____

_____

Day 5

_____

_____

_____

_____

Day 6

_____

_____

_____

_____

Day 7

_____

_____

_____

_____

Week 40

GOD'S DIVINE TIMING

*"To every thing there is a season, and a time to
every purpose under the heaven."*

ECCLESIASTES 3:1

Have you ever experienced a season of waiting on the Lord for
something? Maybe you've been patiently waiting for a while, and
it seems God has been holding out on you. Perhaps you've seen
other people receiving what you've been hoping to receive and feel
discouraged. I've had seasons of waiting and tried to take matters
into my own hands, thinking it was up to me to speed up the process. My attempts to help God always turned out to be futile.

I've learned that as long as God is the center of my life, He will
use every experience I've been through as a lesson to prepare
me for the next season. I don't know what's in my future, but God
knows, and I can trust He wants what's best for me. Rather than
hoping that one day I will arrive at a destination, I've found that
seeing life as a series of seasons helps me remember that God's
timing is intentional. God has brought me into seasons of stillness
to draw me closer to Him, seasons of learning, seasons of reap-
ing fruit, and seasons of dismantling old patterns to build the right
foundation.

Even when we can't see what God is orchestrating behind the
scenes, we can trust that God's timing has a purpose, and we will
reap His blessing in His perfect timing.

ANXIETY RELIEF EXERCISE

Circle of Control (page 180). Think about what is under God's control and what isn't. Entrust everything to God's perfect timing while
remaining obedient to the responsibilities God has given you.

PRAYERS

What are some things that you would like to entrust to God's divine timing?

    Take some time to reflect on the current season in your life. How would you describe the current season you're in?

Day 1

_____

_____

_____

_____

_____

Day 2

_____

_____

_____

_____

_____

Day 3

_____

_____

_____

_____

_____

Day 4

Day 5

Day 6

Day 7

Week 41

CHALLENGING ASSUMPTIONS

"Beloved, believe not every spirit, but try the spirits whether they are of God: because many false prophets are gone out into the world."

1 JOHN 4:1

It's easy to let a thought enter our mind without vetting it and accept it as truth. We can hear something and take it to heart without even realizing it. If these thoughts are lies, they can fester in our mind, take us captive, and trigger our anxiety. Many of the lies we allow in can seem believable because they pose as half-truths.

A lot of the work my clients and I put in together involves testing their assumptions and beliefs against God's Word. When a client comes to sort out the lies that have been keeping them in bondage, their entire disposition changes because they have been set free by the truth.

When we intentionally test every incoming message, our thoughts naturally begin to align with God's heart. In this way, our inner lie detector becomes more accurate over time. When we remain close to God, the Holy Spirit will let us know if something is not aligned with the truth.

ANXIETY RELIEF EXERCISE

Reality Testing (page 193). In this week's exercise, you will examine any assumptions in the stories that you've been telling yourself and realign yourself with the truth.

PRAYERS

Take some time to observe and reflect on any assumptions that you have about yourself, others, God, and the world. What assumptions do you need to test against God's Word?

If you experience anxiety this week, take some time to reflect on what assumptions could be triggering your anxious thoughts and bring those to God.

Day 1

_____

_____

_____

_____

_____

Day 2

_____

_____

_____

_____

_____

Day 3

_____

_____

_____

_____

_____

Day 4

_____

_____

_____

_____

Day 5

_____

_____

_____

_____

Day 6

_____

_____

_____

_____

Day 7

_____

_____

_____

_____

Week 42

GOD IS IN THE DETAILS

"I will praise thee; for I am fearfully and wonderfully made: marvellous are thy works; and that my soul knoweth right well."

PSALM 139:14

God is in all the details, no matter how big or small. The Bible is filled with genealogies, prophecies, and intricate details that set up the events leading to Jesus' death, burial, and resurrection.

When it comes to us, God has carefully knit us in our mother's womb. He has orchestrated events in our lives that we are not even aware of until after they occur. Sometimes we miss these details because we are more focused on keeping up with our emails, our five-year plans, and our schedules, but it's important to notice God's work in our life and see how He works out important details.

It can be hard to believe that God truly cares about every detail in our life, but I have experienced His presence in everyday moments. I have felt His presence when I sing praise songs in the shower or listen to the Bible on audio while doing chores. I have felt His presence when I feel compelled to pray for someone or wake up in the morning with peace and calm.

When God works something out, it can feel like a surprising turn of events that would be unexplainable apart from God. God is in the business of doing the impossible and unexpected. When we're fearful because we don't know how something will work out, we can believe that God will work things out in a way that only He can.

ANXIETY RELIEF EXERCISE

Seeing the Good (page 223). Thank God for allowing certain events in your life to unfold the way they did to bring you as far as He has today.

PRAYERS

What are some events that have occurred for you to be where you are today?

What are some details in your life that cause you anxiety to think about because you don't know how they will work out? Take some time this week to ask God to guide you in your next steps.

Day 1

_____

_____

_____

_____

_____

Day 2

_____

_____

_____

_____

Day 3

_____

_____

_____

_____

Day 4

_____

_____

_____

_____

_____

Day 5

_____

_____

_____

_____

_____

Day 6

_____

_____

_____

_____

_____

Day 7

_____

_____

_____

_____

_____

Week 43

EFFECTIVE PRAYER

*"And this is the confidence that we have in him, that, if we
ask any thing according to his will, he heareth us."*

1 JOHN 5:14

Prayer is powerful enough to change the circumstances of a situation and one of the most effective tools we have to combat our anxiety. Many times, I reluctantly prayed during a difficult situation and the Holy Spirit eased my anxiety and gave me a fresh perspective.

Prayer is our spiritual battleground where we fight against the enemy and intercede, or pray, for others. It is an opportunity to partner with God so He can work in us and through us. Three important aspects of effective prayer are:

- an unwavering faith (James 1:6)

- an openness to God's will

- a willingness to lay down our own agenda

When we persist in prayer, we can be confident that God will intervene. Sometimes the answer He gives is a "No" or "Wait," but He will always answer.

ANXIETY RELIEF EXERCISE

Battle Prayers (page 201). This week's exercise will prepare you for when you are feeling flustered or panicked and in need of prayer.

PRAYERS

In what ways have you experienced the power of prayer in your life?

How can you make prayer a greater priority in your life?

Day 1

_____

_____

_____

_____

_____

Day 2

_____

_____

_____

_____

_____

Day 3

_____

_____

_____

_____

_____

Day 4

Day 5

Day 6

Day 7

Week 44
JOY IN THE JOURNEY

"Commit thy works unto the LORD, and thy thoughts shall be established."

PROVERBS 16:3

Making progress toward an outcome involves ups and downs and is usually far from perfect. It's easy to forget to savor the journey and reflect on your internal growth.

Working with clients, I've learned that steps taken gradually and incrementally over time result in the most long-lasting and sustainable changes. We can treat spiritual growth like a diet fad, where we come to a point of arrival then hope to coast, but when this is our approach, we will likely give up in the face of adversity.

When we focus on the outcome of our work, anxiety can flare up, especially when we don't see the fruit of our labor right away. If instead, we commit everything we do unto the Lord, He can help direct our plans and lead us to where we should go. Instead of fixating on the outcome, we can even learn to enjoy the journey. Our job isn't to ensure success, but to entrust the outcome in Him and to be empowered with His grace.

ANXIETY RELIEF EXERCISE

Process Goals (page 185). In this week's exercise, you will identify some small steps that you can take to help focus on moving toward your goals and finding joy in your journey.

PRAYERS

What is God asking you to focus on at this point in your journey? It could be your prayer life, new habits, improving certain skills (e.g., communication), or certain character traits (e.g., patience).

What habits would you like to build to cultivate joy in your life? What steps can you take toward developing these habits? How can you enjoy or savor the process more?

Day 1

_____

_____

_____

_____

Day 2

_____

_____

_____

_____

Day 3

_____

_____

_____

_____

Day 4

Day 5

Day 6

Day 7

Week 45

CLAIMING GOD'S PROMISES

"God is not a man, that he should lie; neither the son of man,
that he should repent: hath he said, and shall he not do it?
or hath he spoken, and shall he not make it good?"

NUMBERS 23:19

We've all probably experienced broken promises at some point in our lives. Putting our trust in people can be difficult when we have experienced hurt and disappointment, but we can trust that God always makes good on His promises.

The promises in God's Word are here for us to claim when we are struggling, when we are seeking guidance, or when we need clarity, hope, and wisdom.

When nothing seems certain, we can remember that God never goes back on His Word or changes His mind. We can hold onto His promises, knowing that they are meant for us. We can recall His promises from Scripture for strength and peace of mind when we are experiencing anxiety.

ANXIETY RELIEF EXERCISE

Battle Verses (page 203). Use this week's exercise to choose verses related to God's promises as a reminder to trust in Him when you feel anxious.

PRAYERS

What does it mean to you that God is a promise keeper?

What are some promises from Scripture you would like to claim today? Choose one to meditate on whenever you experience anxiety throughout the week.

Day 1

_____

_____

_____

_____

_____

Day 2

_____

_____

_____

_____

_____

Day 3

_____

_____

_____

_____

_____

Day 4

_____

_____

_____

_____

_____

Day 5

_____

_____

_____

_____

_____

Day 6

_____

_____

_____

_____

_____

Day 7

_____

_____

_____

_____

_____

Week 46

MISTAKING THE CAUSE AND THE EFFECT

"For by grace are ye saved through faith; and that Not of yourselves: it is the gift of God: not of works, lest any man should boast."

EPHESIANS 2:8–9

God's grace is a gift that cannot be earned by our good deeds. Rather, good deeds are an overflow or effect of receiving God's grace. A common trap is treating God's grace as transactional— mistaking God's favor as a reward for our efforts and hard work.

For example, we may believe that attending church and completing a checklist that involves reading the Bible and praying daily for thirty minutes means earning God's grace. While reading the Bible regularly is a very important habit, it's also important to examine the true motive behind why we are studying the Bible. Guilt or self-righteousness can be the reasons for why we stick to our Bible study routine rather than a true desire to encounter Jesus. If we are studying God's Word with different motivations, we are likely to focus on how well we can stick to a routine and fall into a performative form of religion.

When we fall into these traps, we put a greater focus on our own works and rely on ourselves, rather than relying on God's grace to perform the work He empowers us to do. True transformation comes from God's grace, not our ability to complete a daily checklist. When we recognize that receiving grace is an unmerited favor in our lives, then we can respond with gratitude, praise, and willing obedience.

ANXIETY RELIEF EXERCISE

Reality Testing (page 193). Legalistic thinking can sometimes fall into the form of "If I do *X*, then I will be or get *Y*." Use this week's exercise to identify whether you're falling into any type of legalistic thinking.

PRAYERS

In what areas of your life have you mistaken an effect for a cause?

Day 1

_____

_____

_____

_____

_____

Day 2

_____

_____

_____

_____

_____

Day 3

_____

_____

_____

_____

_____

Day 4

Day 5

Day 6

Day 7

Week 47

NEW TERRITORY

"But as for you, ye thought evil against me; but God meant it unto good, to bring to pass, as it is this day, to save much people alive."

GENESIS 50:20

In the Bible, Joseph, the son of Jacob, went through many trials and traumatic events. He felt alone and forgotten because his eleven brothers betrayed him. However, when the difficult part of his journey came to pass, he saw that God was able to use every challenge for good.

The enemy will attempt to derail us, especially when we're keen to serve God. As a life coach, I've spoken to many women who've questioned their faith because they encountered so much opposition and endured so many hardships in their lives. The enemy will try to persuade us that we're too broken and weak to be used by God. If we allow opposition to stop us, we disqualify ourselves from what God has called us to do and can miss out an opportunity to serve God.

I've experienced dark valleys many times, and I became discouraged and feared getting hurt, but God encouraged me to remain faithful and obedient. When I reached the hill on the other side, I realized God was using the trial to prepare me for what was next.

ANXIETY RELIEF EXERCISE

Seeing the Good (page 223). When we experience a valley, it can feel like we will be stuck there forever. Use this week's exercise to think of when God used a valley to help strengthen your faith and prepare you for bigger responsibilities.

PRAYERS

What challenges have you experienced that appeared to be an obstacle but ended up resulting in something good? The next time you experience opposition, read over these experiences for encouragement.

Day 1

_____

_____

_____

_____

_____

Day 2

_____

_____

_____

_____

_____

Day 3

_____

_____

_____

_____

_____

Day 4

_____

_____

_____

_____

_____

Day 5

_____

_____

_____

_____

Day 6

_____

_____

_____

_____

Day 7

_____

_____

_____

_____

Week 48

GOD'S VANTAGE POINT

"For my thoughts are not your thoughts, neither are your ways my ways, saith the LORD. For as the heavens are higher than the earth, so are my ways higher than your ways, and my thoughts than your thoughts."

ISAIAH 55:8–9

The human brain struggles to fathom the fact that God is all knowing and all powerful. I realize my own limits whenever I think about how God created all the galaxies in the universe. Human nature compels us to know everything, but the longer I walk with God, the more I am humbled about how much I don't know.

From our human perspective, following Jesus can seem illogical and impractical. He may ask us to go somewhere or do something we never imagined doing or thought was possible. He may ask us to love and serve people in a way that we wouldn't have been able to in our own strength.

My limited thinking often leads to anxiety. I'm sure that my worries seem very silly from God's vantage point. By my calculations, a resolution to my problems can seem impossible. But when I remember that His thoughts, methods, and plans are far beyond my comprehension, I know that God's plan is bigger and better than I could ever imagine. God shows me glimpses of the big picture but wants me to trust Him with the rest. His vantage point is infinitely bigger, and I accept that He knows what's best for me. Our view is limited, but His is not.

ANXIETY RELIEF EXERCISE

Replace Lies and Meditate on Truths (page 194). Recognize your human limitations. Remember that God's thoughts and plans are way bigger.

PRAYERS

Take some time to reflect on any negative thoughts you have been having. Ask God to help you see things from His vantage point or to trust that things will come together the way it's meant to.

Day 1

_____
_____
_____
_____
_____

Day 2

_____
_____
_____
_____

Day 3

_____
_____
_____
_____

Day 4

_____
_____
_____
_____
_____

Day 5

_____
_____
_____
_____
_____

Day 6

_____
_____
_____
_____
_____

Day 7

_____
_____
_____
_____
_____

Week 49

BUT IF NOT

"If it be so, our God whom we serve is able to deliver us from the burning fiery furnace, and he will deliver us out of thine hand, O king. But if not, be it known unto thee, O king, that we will not serve thy gods, nor worship the golden image which thou hast set up."

DANIEL 3:17–18

Despite being threatened to be thrown into a fiery furnace by the Babylonian king, Shadrach, Meshach, and Abednego remained faithful to God by refusing to bow down before a gold idol. Instead, they responded to the threats by declaring that God could save them from the fire, and even if He did not, they would remain faithful to their God. Although the three were thrown into the fire, they were completely unharmed.

Even in desperate circumstances, accepting our fate no matter what happens is freeing. This doesn't mean we will not experience fear or anxiety, but we can stand boldly in our faith. We have a choice to not give in to our fear. Regardless of what we encounter in our lives, we can put our hope in Jesus, knowing that He will never leave or forsake us. Even though Shadrach, Meshach, and Abednego were going to be thrown into the fire, they did not compromise and bow down to the idol because they knew God would be with them. In the same way, no matter what we face, we can know Jesus will be there.

ANXIETY RELIEF EXERCISE

Battle Prayers (page 201). For this week's exercise, revisit your battle prayers in preparation of facing the enemy's temptations.

PRAYERS

Have you ever experienced this kind of bold faith? Have you trusted in God even when you knew things might not turn out how you hoped or expected?

The next time you encounter a situation that requires faith in God's deliverance, try this prayer: *"God, I know You are able to deliver me. But if not, I am still willing to trust in You."*

Day 1

_____

_____

_____

_____

_____

Day 2

_____

_____

_____

_____

Day 3

_____

_____

_____

_____

Day 4

_____
_____
_____
_____
_____

Day 5

_____
_____
_____
_____
_____

Day 6

_____
_____
_____
_____

Day 7

_____
_____
_____
_____

Week 50

GOD'S PERFECT LOVE

"There is no fear in love; but perfect love casteth out fear: because fear hath torment. He that feareth is not made perfect in love."

1 JOHN 4:18

When there is a lack of trust in a relationship, fear, anxiety, and depression are usually lurking. Our self-protective instincts kick in, and we experience fight-or-flight responses where we lash out or run away from our problems.

God's love is perfect, meaning it's unconditional and can be trusted. Even after I accepted Jesus as my Savior, it was still difficult for me to fully comprehend the unconditional nature of His love. My perception of love was based on tainted, conditional human love. I could not grasp how God's love could be so perfect and pure. Over time, I started to learn what it meant to allow God to love me. His love has changed my heart and my response to difficult challenges in my life. When I understand that He loves me, I no longer have fear because I know God has my back.

ANXIETY RELIEF EXERCISE

Receiving God's Love and Compassion (page 216). In this week's exercise, reflect on the attributes of God's love while you open your heart to receive and embrace it.

PRAYERS

Have you ever resisted or found it difficult to receive God's love?

How does it feel to know that God has your back?

How would you describe God's love?

Day 1

_____

_____

_____

_____

_____

Day 2

_____

_____

_____

_____

_____

Day 3

_____

_____

_____

_____

_____

Day 4

_____

_____

_____

_____

_____

Day 5

_____

_____

_____

_____

_____

Day 6

_____

_____

_____

_____

_____

Day 7

_____

_____

_____

_____

_____

Week 51
FREEDOM IN FORGIVENESS

"Follow peace with all men, and holiness, without which no man shall see the Lord: Looking diligently lest any man fail of the grace of God; lest any root of bitterness springing up trouble you, and thereby many be defiled."

HEBREWS 12:14–15

Corrie ten Boom was a Christian woman who, along with her family, was arrested for hiding Dutch Jews in their home from the Nazis during World War II. Four of her family members, including her sister, passed away while being imprisoned. In her book, *Tramp for the Lord*, Corrie describes how God called her to "tramp" across the world after the war to share her story and teach others about God's forgiveness of sins. One day, at a church in Munich, she encountered a former Nazi guard who had been stationed at the concentration camp where her sister Betsie had died. He was one of the cruelest guards at the concentration camp but had since become a Christian. He asked Corrie ten Boom for her forgiveness. She couldn't forgive him on her own; only God's grace could make it possible, so she cried to the Lord for help. She teared up as she felt warmth and healing from the Lord. She was then able to genuinely tell the man she forgave him.

When we don't forgive others, bitterness can grow in our heart as a poisonous root and steal our peace. Unforgiveness can even make us physically sick. When we harbor negative feelings toward someone, stress and anxiety can overwhelm us. When we forgive, we can be freed from the resentment that can overtake our heart. When we understand that God forgives and treats us as if He no longer remembers our sins, we can do that for others as well (Hebrews 10:17). If we have a hard time forgiving, God can give us the strength to forgive the way He gave Corrie the ability to forgive.

ANXIETY RELIEF EXERCISE

Letter Writing (page 225). You can receive God's help to forgive those who have hurt you. In this week's exercise, express and process any feelings of hurt and disappointment and give them unto the Lord.

PRAYERS

Have you been harboring any negative feelings toward anyone? Ask God to help you forgive them.

Day 1

_____

_____

_____

_____

_____

Day 2

_____

_____

_____

_____

_____

Day 3

_____

_____

_____

_____

_____

Day 4

_____

_____

_____

_____

_____

Day 5

_____

_____

_____

_____

_____

Day 6

_____

_____

_____

_____

_____

Day 7

_____

_____

_____

_____

_____

Week 52

PEACE OF MIND

*"Thou wilt keep him in perfect peace, whose mind is
stayed on thee: because he trusteth in thee."*

ISAIAH 26:3

Peace is a fruit of the Spirit that is cultivated by abiding in God's presence. It is hard to remain at peace when we experience difficult trials, but trials are the grounds for training and testing our faith. When we are willing to have our faith tested, our faith is strengthened as we actively rely on God and fight our battles with Him.

God promises to give us perfect peace if we keep our mind on Him, no matter what we are going through. When we trust in Him, we do not have anything to fear, and we are not easily swept away by our anxious thoughts.

ANXIETY RELIEF EXERCISE

Hearing from God through Scripture (page 224). In this week's exercise, you will be able to rely on the truths in God's Word to renew and guard your mind with peace.

PRAYERS

When do you find it difficult to keep your eyes focused on God?

When was a time you experienced God's peace even when you were going through a challenging time in your life? How can this experience encourage you in the future?

Day 1

_____

_____

_____

_____

_____

Day 2

_____

_____

_____

_____

_____

Day 3

_____

_____

_____

_____

_____

Day 4

_____

_____

_____

_____

_____

Day 5

_____

_____

_____

_____

_____

Day 6

_____

_____

_____

_____

_____

Day 7

_____

_____

_____

_____

_____

Part Two

ANXIETY RELIEF EXERCISES

This section comprises 25 exercises that include actionable strategies that can help you manage your anxiety. These skills and exercises are essential for staying grounded in Christ, turning to God and focusing on Him, exploring and understanding your thoughts and feelings, and setting goals and action plans.

Please note that these exercises are not meant to be prescriptive but are intended to provide you with flexible strategies you can use again and again. Modify or adapt any of them in a way that works best for you.

IDENTITY-BASED SCRIPTURE DECLARATIONS

Useful for: grounding yourself and your identity in Christ, overcoming self-criticism, managing intrusive thoughts

Time: 30 minutes

Sometimes our anxiety is caused by a shaming or condemning voice in our head that constantly tells us we're not doing enough and that we are sure to fail. Instead of allowing our Creator to define us, we may have tied our worth to something else, like our work. When we are secure in our true identity in Christ, we can operate from God's strength and grace. Scriptures about our identity remind us of who we are: beloved daughters of the King. Bible verses help raise our awareness of how God empowers us to become all He has called us to be. This exercise will help ground yourself in your identity in Christ and avoid being consumed by the inner critic in your mind.

---

1. Take a few deep, slow breaths to quiet your mind.

2. Read over the declarations and think about their meaning.

3. Read the related Scriptures for any statements that stand out to you.

4. Read the declarations and Scriptures as needed throughout the day.

   I am a beloved daughter of God. (Galatians 3:26; 1 John 3:1; Romans 8:15)

I am fearfully and wonderfully made in the image of God. (Psalm 139:14; Genesis 1:26–27)

I am forgiven, redeemed, and accepted by God. (1 John 1:9; Galatians 4:5; Ephesians 1:6–7)

I am free from condemnation. (Romans 8:1)

I am unconditionally loved and precious to God. (John 3:16; 1 John 4:19; Matthew 10:29–31; 1 Corinthians 6:20)

I am never abandoned or separated from God's love. (John 6:37; Hebrews 13:5; Romans 8:38–39)

I am empowered by God's grace which gives me strength. (2 Corinthians 12:9; Philippians 4:13)

I am a royal heir with Christ. (1 Peter 2:9; Galatians 3:29; Romans 8:17)

I am more than a conqueror. (Romans 8:37)

I am God's workmanship. (Ephesians 2:10)

Tip:

Record the identity-based declarations and related Scriptures in a voice note, a note app, or index cards for easy access when you notice self-condemning thoughts arising.

CIRCLE OF CONTROL

Useful for: when you're worried about the outcome of a situation

Time: 10–20 minutes, as often as needed

Sometimes anxiety can be caused by worrying about the aspects of a situation that we are unable to control. We play a role and have responsibility in any situation we are involved in, and while God wants us to take responsibility for certain things, other times He wants us to leave it up to His control. Oftentimes, the concerns that we are most worried about are the things that are in God's realm of responsibility, not ours. When we understand our limits, we can focus on what is up to us to take care of and leave the rest up to God. When we try to control things that are not in our jurisdiction, we often neglect to focus on what God is asking us to do.

Through this exercise, you can express your worries to God. The main goal of this exercise is to help you refocus on the things God is asking you to be responsible for, so that you can entrust everything else to His control.

---

1. Ask God to help you view your situation objectively as you complete this exercise.

2. Take some time to reflect on a concern or situation you're worried about. Write out how you feel about the situation, what you're worried about, and what outcome you're fearing.

3. Write down everything about the situation that is and isn't in your control. One place to start is remembering that you

are responsible for your own thoughts, feelings, actions, and responses, while others are responsible for their own.

4. Identify one action step you can take from under your realm of responsibility.

5. Ask God to help you take this action step and trust Him for everything else in His control.

Tip:

It's very normal to cast your cares onto God then catch yourself taking back what you've submitted to His control. When this happens, remind yourself of God's power; you can give what you're worried about to Him again, as many times as it takes!

PROCESS GOALS

Useful for: overcoming procrastination, setting goals, prioritizing responsibilities, finding motivation, and when you're feeling overwhelmed with tasks.

Time: 30–60 minutes for the first planning session; review goals for five minutes as often as needed

As Christians, we are called to be responsible stewards of everything we have. This means using our body, time, resources, and gifts for God's glory. God may be calling us toward specific goals in certain seasons of our lives. However, thinking about our goals can feel overwhelming, especially when we haven't thought about how we might achieve them. For example, if we have a general goal of improving our health, it's difficult to start when we haven't thought about what actions and behaviors are required to get there. We can set a goal to lose a certain amount of weight by a certain date, but weight fluctuations can result from several different factors, some of which are not entirely in our control.

Of course, we don't need to map out exactly every step since we can trust God to help us work out the details, but we can engage in everyday actions and behaviors that are within our realm of responsibility, ultimately bringing us closer to achieving our goals.

This exercise will help you come up with *process goals* or certain actions and behaviors that can help you on your journey toward achieving your goals.

1. Start with a prayer asking God to help direct your steps.

2. Do a brain dump and write down different things you believe you are being called by God to achieve.

3. If the number of things on your list feels overwhelming, sort each goal into categories (e.g., spiritual, health, personal, finance, work, relationships).

4. Come up with goals that are specific and measurable through tracking or quantified ways.

5. Attach attainable and realistic measurables for each goal so you can easily track your progress.

6. Choose one to three process goals to work on for a set time frame (e.g., a month).

7. Here are some examples:

   GOAL CATEGORY: Health (e.g., being more active)
   GOAL: I will do something active (e.g., walk, go the gym, Pilates) for at least 30 minutes per day, three times a week, for the next month.

   GOAL CATEGORY: Family (e.g., being more present with my family)
   GOAL: For the next three weeks, I will put my phone away at 7:00 p.m. every evening so I can focus on spending time with my family.

8. During the trial period, reflect and jot down what obstacles you experienced, what benefits you experienced, what you learned during the trial period, and whether you'd like to adjust your goals.

Tip:

- If you find that you can't always accomplish everything you set out to do, allow yourself grace. Completing 10 percent of something you set out to achieve is still an accomplishment. There will be ups and downs. Remember that you can rely on God to give you the strength to keep going. Be open to readjusting your plans and course correcting. What you learn from the process is very important for your progress.

- If you are pursuing a goal with no guaranteed outcome, remind yourself that God will guide you, even when things don't turn out the way you expect. Take some time to meditate on Proverbs 16:9.

  A man's heart deviseth his way: but the LORD directeth his steps. (Proverbs 16:9)

- Look for multiple signs of progress and avoid being tied to a narrow set of expectations of what your progress must look like. We can easily become discouraged when we fixate on only one outcome (e.g., how much weight we've lost, the number of dollars in our bank account). So rather than basing your health and diet goals on how much weight you've lost on the scale, gauge how much stronger you feel from resistance training, how much more energy you have from eating nutrient-dense foods, or how much your anxiety levels have reduced as a result of an active and healthy lifestyle.

SMALL STEPS

Useful for: overcoming procrastination, when you're feeling overwhelmed with tasks

Time: 15 minutes, as often as needed

This exercise will help you break down any goal or task into smaller steps. You may have a high-priority task that feels overwhelming, like cleaning the house. Procrastination often occurs when we feel overwhelmed because the task at hand seems too large. Breaking things down into the tiniest possible steps can help alleviate overwhelming feelings.

---

1. Establish a calm and peaceful environment. You can make yourself your favorite drink, light a candle, find your favorite blanket, or put on a praise song you love.

2. Select a goal or task that you'd like to focus on.

3. Break the goal or task down into multiple, small steps. For example, if your goal is to do something active such as going for a walk, then it could require the following steps:

   a. schedule time to walk

   b. change into active clothes

   c. fill up your water bottle

   d. put on your walking shoes

   e. go outside

   f. walk

4. Set aside time to work on your goal.

5. Begin working on the task. If you gain momentum, keep going.

6. If you don't feel like working on your goal after five minutes, take some time to reflect on what is causing resistance. Ask God to help you overcome the discomfort.

7. If you still find that the task is too difficult, seek support from others, collect more information and/or research to bolster your action plan. For example, if you have a goal of increasing your physical activity, you can research nearby hiking trails or enlist a walking buddy.

8. Take regular breaks to stretch and regain focus. You can start by taking five-to-ten-minute breaks every 25 minutes. A timer or a time management app can be a helpful tool for this exercise.

Tip:

If you find that you are experiencing a lot of resistance as you complete certain tasks, a deep-seated belief could be driving your fear and anxiety. If you need help identifying what these beliefs might be, refer to Exercises Expressive Journaling (page 187), Explore Your Thoughts and Feeling (page 189), Faulty Thinking Traps (page 191). You can also journal about your feelings to help illuminate the reason behind your resistance and help you move forward.

EXPRESSIVE JOURNALING

Useful for: identifying what you're thinking and feeling, acknowledging difficult emotions

time: as long as you need, as often as you need

Sometimes we feel a mix of emotions that cause us to feel discombobulated and anxious. If you're feeling this way, it can be helpful to take the time to express these emotions to God. Expressive journaling can help you sort out and examine your feelings. Bring them to God so He can help you process what you're feeling.

---

1. Ask God to help you identify what you're feeling and why.

2. Write down what you're feeling on a piece of paper or in a journal. Try not to censor yourself while writing down your feelings.

3. For each emotion, complete the prompt, *"I acknowledge that I feel [emotion] because . . ."*

4. Take each of your emotions to God in prayer using the following prompt: *"Lord, I give you my [e.g., fear, resentment, anger] about x."*

Tip:

- It can be difficult to identify your emotions, especially if you're not used to this practice. Becoming familiar with your own emotions takes time. The more practice, the easier it will become to acknowledge and manage them over time.

- If you're having trouble identifying what you're feeling, look up a wheel of emotions online as a guide to help determine the specific emotions you're feeling. It is important to learn to recognize what you are feeling because it can help you figure out what's really going on and respond appropriately. Use more specific terms that describe your emotions (e.g., guilty, offended, amazed) rather than saying, "I feel good" or, "I feel bad." You can also observe the sensations you feel in your body and take note of them.

EXPLORE YOUR THOUGHTS AND FEELINGS

Useful for: processing what you're feeling

Time: as long and often as you need

This exercise is designed to help you explore your thoughts and feelings with the help of the Holy Spirit.

---

1. Take a few slow, deep breaths to restore your body to a calmer state.

2. Observe different thoughts and feelings you've been experiencing. You can keep a journal to record these thoughts and feelings throughout the week.

3. Circle the thoughts and emotions that you felt the strongest. You can draw pictures, write labels (e.g., anxiety) and circle them, or any other way that helps you keep track of them.

4. With compassionate curiosity, spend some time exploring these thoughts and feelings, as you would with a close friend or someone you care about. Or, share what you've been thinking and feeling with a trusted person. Here are some examples of questions to ask:

   • What happened?

   • How did I interpret what happened?

- Am I experiencing this emotion because I'm afraid something will happen? If so, what is it? Can I share these fears with God?

- Am I responding this way because there's something I'm trying to protect myself from or run away from? If so, what is it?

- Can I ask God to help me handle the situation appropriately?

- Do I have a need that is not being met? Can I ask God to help meet these unmet needs?

Tip

Feel free to come up with your own questions to help you dig deeper and gain a better understanding of what is happening under the surface. The Holy Spirit will point your attention to certain things to help guide you.

FAULTY THINKING TRAPS

Useful for: identifying faulty thinking traps

Time: Five minutes a day for journaling, plus 30 minutes for the remaining portion of the exercise

The stories we tell ourselves repeatedly have a powerful impact. They can either make us feel deflated and discouraged or inspired and motivated. Identifying faulty thinking traps can help weed out the stories that are dictating our thoughts, feelings, and behaviors.

When we begin to examine what we've been telling ourselves over and over again, certain behavior patterns begin to make sense. Identifying our faulty thinking traps will help increase our awareness of their presence and help us see that we have a choice in how we respond to them. With this knowledge, we can evaluate how they impact us and ask God to help us break free and replace the traps with truth.

---

1. Keep a journal of your thoughts and feelings and update it regularly. If you want more guidance and prompts to help you with this step, review Expressive Journaling (page 187) and Explore Your Thoughts and Feelings (page 189).

2. Based on what you've learned from journaling, identify any stories you've been frequently telling yourself. Some of these stories will be half-truths, some you've learned in a previous context, and some are beliefs that helped you survive difficult situations in the past. Here are some examples of common stories we tell ourselves:

- *I am never going to be good enough.*

- *Nothing good ever happens to me.*

- *The worst is going to happen.*

- *I can't trust anyone.*

- *I am going to fail.*

- *I will never have enough time and money.*

- *God cares more about others than me.*

- *If I want things to go my way, I must handle it myself.*

- *God is constantly punishing me.*

- *I have to do what others expect of me or no one will accept me.*

- *I have to do everything by myself or no one else will do it.*

- *As long as I do what others want, I will be safe.*

3. Examine the stories you've been telling yourself. How have these stories affected you and your life?

Tip:

- Don't rush the process. Don't worry about your progress. Trust His timing. He will bring focus on what needs attention.

- To better recognize faulty thinking traps, reflect on where you learned it. They may be related to beliefs formed in your life (e.g., childhood or significant events) that impacted you deeply.

REALITY TESTING

Useful for: recognizing and examining faulty thinking traps

Time: 30–60 minutes

In this exercise, examine the stories you've been thinking about and check them against reality. Testing the stories can help you recognize what lies are feeding these faulty thinking traps. The enemy can use these lies to draw you away from God and what He has called you to do.

---

1. Identify and examine the stories you've been telling yourself. If you need examples to help you with this step, review Exercise Faulty Thinking Traps (page 191) first.

2. Answer the following questions about them:

    •   What evidence supports the story I'm telling myself?

    •   Is there a false narrative I am believing? Have I made a connection between things that aren't really related?

    •   Where might I be taking an extreme stance in my thinking?

3. Ask God to help reveal parts of the story you need to release and what truths you need His help to accept. Reflect and note any insights you have discovered.

    Tip

    When the intensity of our emotions are strong, it is better to wait until we can be more objective and clear-headed about our thinking traps.

REPLACE LIES AND MEDITATE ON TRUTHS

Useful for: replacing thinking traps with God's truths

Time: Approximately 30–60 minutes to create the list of truths; then use for five minutes as often as needed

In this exercise, you will have the opportunity to identify thinking traps and replace those lies with biblical truths.

---

1. Review Reality Testing (page 193) before proceeding.

2. Identify any lies that fuel some of your thinking patterns. Write these on a piece of paper.

3. Ask God to help you see what truths can be used to combat each of these lies.

4. Select a Bible verse that is relevant to each lie. You can use Bible verses from the weekly devotions in this book or look up Bible verses on the relevant topic online.

5. Reframe and write a truth statement for each lie based on the biblical truth on a separate note.

6. Take the paper with the lies written on it and rip it up into pieces.

7. Keep your truth statements somewhere visible (e.g., phone wallpaper, Post-its on bathroom mirror).

8. Meditate on the truth statements and look up the relevant Bible verses whenever you catch yourself in a thinking trap and as often as needed.

9. Here are some examples:

THINKING TRAP: I am a failure and can't do anything right.
BIBLICAL TRUTH: I can rely on God's grace to empower and strengthen me.
RELEVANT BIBLE VERSES: 2 Corinthians 12:9; Philippians 2:13

THINKING TRAP: I have to worry about my future.
BIBLICAL TRUTH: God knows what I need, and He will take care of me.
RELEVANT BIBLE VERSES: Romans 8:32; Philippians 4:19; Matthew 6:32–33; Psalm 37:4

THINKING TRAP: I must do everything perfectly to be worthy of love.
BIBLICAL TRUTH: God loves me unconditionally as His daughter regardless of what I do.
RELEVANT BIBLE VERSES: John 3:16; 1 John 3:1; Romans 8:38–39; John 6:37; 1 John 4:19

REPLACE NEGATIVE HABITS

Useful for: identifying anxiety-related triggers for negative habits, building new, healthy habits

Time: as much time as needed, as often as needed

Anxiety and shame can trigger destructive habits and lead to an unhealthy cycle. Oftentimes, we engage in these behaviors because we have an unmet need, and instead of turning to God for help, we turn to counterfeit comforts.

There can be some common triggers that set off a habitual response that you perceive will lead to a reward or benefit. Some behaviors involve undesired actions like addictive habits, emotionally lashing out at others, or it might be turning to food for comfort when experiencing a certain emotion. This exercise will help you identify the triggers and rewards for certain negative habits.

Recognizing these actions can help us understand why we keep engaging in bad habits. When we can recognize our triggers, we can learn to replace old habits with new ones.

---

1. Choose one unhelpful habit to monitor for a set time period (e.g., two weeks).

2. **DATE AND TIME:** Write down the date and time when you notice yourself falling into the habit. Note whether it seems to mostly fall on a particular time or day of the week. If some time has passed since you engaged in the habit and you didn't record it instantly, that's okay—you can still record it.

3. **WHAT HAPPENED IMMEDIATELY BEFORE:** Write down what you were thinking, feeling, and doing before you engaged in the habit and what else was happening or who you were with (e.g., I was bored, I was anxious about my workload, I was exhausted, someone said something hurtful).

4. **REWARD OR BENEFIT:** Write down what benefit you were hoping to achieve from the unhelpful habit or what unmet need you were seeking to satisfy (e.g., feeling more relaxed, avoiding facing a fear, looking for approval, love or connection).

5. **IDENTIFY TRIGGERS:** Look for any patterns of triggers that occur frequently and are tied to the habit.

6. **FIND A REPLACEMENT:** Ask God to help you find a good replacement for the negative habit (e.g., listening to Christian audiobooks instead of excessive social media consumption). This habit should be something that spiritually replenishes you instead of drains you.

7. **TRY THE REPLACEMENT:** Test the replacement habit for a trial period (e.g., one month). Write down any challenges and adjust as needed. You can start to stack new healthy habits once you get comfortable with each new habit.

Tip:

Building a new habit will take time. Recruit an accountability partner to share new habits you are setting out to develop.

ACKNOWLEDGING YOUR EMOTIONS

Useful for: dealing with difficult emotions

Time: 20 minutes, as often as needed

Sometimes we can become so blended with our emotional responses that it's difficult to separate what we're feeling from the truth. We can easily believe that whatever we're feeling or thinking must be true.

If we let our emotions automatically dictate our reality, we can reinforce these responses. For example, whenever we are feeling anxious about something, we may feel a heightened sense of danger and use avoidance to cope with the feelings we are experiencing. Avoidance gives us the benefit of not having to deal with difficult challenges, but dealing with everything in this way can lead to detrimental consequences (e.g., avoiding looking at bills because they make you feel anxious).

However, we can acknowledge our emotions and try to understand them in a way that helps us understand ourselves better so that we don't respond in reactive ways. Rather than criticizing ourselves for what we're feeling, we can approach our emotions with compassionate curiosity. For example, we may want to take some time to try to understand why opening bills makes us feel anxious. We do not have to agree with everything our emotions are saying, but rather than using avoidance tactics, we can bring these emotions to God.

If we learn to turn to God when we experience difficult emotions, we can rely on the Holy Spirit to give us empathy and guide our response to our emotions. While emotions can be helpful messengers, they don't need to have control over us. This exercise is designed to help you acknowledge your emotions, remind you that you are not your emotions, and that God can help you respond to them appropriately.

---

1. Pause and observe what is going on in your body (e.g., tightness in your chest) and mind (e.g., confusion).

2. Identify and write down what emotions you are feeling and why you are feeling them. If you're having trouble identifying what you're feeling, review Expressive Journaling (page 187).

3. Read the following truths whenever you need help separating yourself from your feelings. Feel free to adjust as needed.

   - *I am experiencing emotions, but I am not my emotions.*

   - *I may be feeling anxiety, but I am not anxiety.*

   - *I am not my emotional reactions. I am a daughter of God.*

   - *I am not the anxiety I feel. I am a daughter of God.*

   - *I can share my emotions with God, and He will listen to me.*

   - *God can help me understand and respond to my emotions appropriately.*

   - *I can acknowledge my emotions without being controlled by them.*

   - *God is healing and renewing my mind.*

- *As a daughter of God, I can immerse myself in the truth of God's Word.*

- *I can choose not to listen to the lies of the enemy.*

- *I am free in Christ.*

- *I can process my emotions with God.*

- *God is healing me from my past wounds.*

- *God will give me the strength I need to not be reactive.*

4. Ask God to help you evaluate your emotions appropriately.

Avoid condemning yourself for what you are feeling. Allow the Holy Spirit to help you see the truth about your emotions with compassionate curiosity. Repressing our feelings can be problematic because they can increase in intensity if left ignored. It's important to acknowledge them before we choose how to respond to them.

BATTLE PRAYERS

Useful for: dealing with difficult thoughts and feelings

Time: one week to collect prayers, then use as often as needed

When we experience anxiety, the enemy can try to use our vulnerabilities to push us away from God so we turn to unhealthy coping habits. In this world, we are fighting a spiritual battle that requires spiritual weapons, including prayer. This exercise will help you build a habit of prayer to experience victory over the battles in your mind.

---

1. Write out your prayers for at least one week as you deal with different situations.

2. After the week, choose your favorite prayers to put on index cards, in your phone, or somewhere that's easily and visually accessible to help you when you're experiencing different thoughts, feelings, or situations.

   Example:

   > Dear Heavenly Father,
   > I cast my anxiety and give it all to You. Please help me overcome my fear. Please fill my mind with peace and comfort. Please strengthen me and empower me with Your grace. Please guard my mind from the lies of the enemy and renew my mind with the truth in Your Word.

3. When you start to feel anxious, pull out a prayer card and ask God to help you find victory over your intrusive thoughts.

Tip

You can also keep a list of people (friends, neighbors, those that are ill, leaders, missionaries, ministries, etc.) to pray for to help you avoid being engulfed by your emotions.

BATTLE VERSES

Useful for: dealing with difficult thoughts and feelings

Time: 30–60 minutes to make the list, then use as often as needed

The Bible calls God's Word the Sword of the Spirit because it is an effective means to win our battles. This exercise will equip you to handle your battles by preparing Scripture verses to have during difficult situations.

---

1. Ask God to help you identify battle verses to help you to spiritual victory. Here are some themes and sample Scripture references to help you get started.

   HEALING
   Psalm 34:18
   Psalm 147:3

   COURAGE, STRENGTH, AND PROTECTION
   2 Timothy 1:7
   Philippians 4:13
   Psalm 28:7
   Romans 8:31
   Ephesians 6:10
   Psalm 56:3
   Joshua 1:9

PROVISION

Philippians 4:19

Ephesians 3:20

Romans 8:28

TRIALS AND TEMPTATION

James 1:2–4

1 Corinthians 10:13

2 Corinthians 10:5

GOD'S GRACE

2 Corinthians 12:9

Hebrews 4:16

2. Write your battle verses on index cards and put them on a key ring or in a jar that you can pick out of throughout the day.

Tip

It can be very helpful to memorize your battle verses so they are easily accessible. Try starting with one at a time.

"PICK ME UP" LIST

Useful for: grounding when feeling anxious

Time: approximately 20 minutes to create the list, then use as often as needed

A "Pick Me Up" list is comprised of items you can do when you feel anxious. You can include activities that will help you feel grounded, emotionally safe, and reconnect you with God and others.

---

1. Take an inventory of activities that give you a sense of peace and calm.

2. When feeling anxious, choose something on the list to ground you. If the first thing you try on the list doesn't help, try something else.

3. Whenever you find another "Pick Me Up" activity that's not on the list, add it.

4. Here are some actions that you can put on your "Pick Me Up" list:

Connecting with a good friend

Spending time with a pet

Taking a short walk

Breathing deeply and slowly

Doing a full body stretch

Journaling

Praying/being still and having a conversation with God

Reading the Bible

Listening to/singing a favorite worship song

Putting on a sermon

Doing a creative hobby (e.g., painting/coloring, knitting, playing a musical instrument)

Reading or listening to audiobooks/podcasts

Giving or receiving a hug

Dancing

Making or ordering your favorite food, drink, or snack

Reciting and meditating on your favorite Bible verses

Watching a sunrise or sunset

Talking with a therapist, mentor, life coach

Reading a favorite devotional

Gardening

Star gazing

Taking a bath or nap

GIVING GOD YOUR WORRIES AND FEARS

Useful for: overwhelming feelings, submitting fears and worries to God

Time: 30 minutes, as often as needed

In this exercise, you will identify, express, and evaluate your fears and worries, so you can give them to God and remove their power over you. When we closely examine what worries us, it can help us see our situation more objectively. Writing out everything we're afraid of and looking at all our fears on paper can help us see that they are much more manageable than we anticipated.

---

1. Start with a prayer asking God for clarity, peace, and guidance as you complete this exercise.

2. Write down all the fears and worries currently occupying your mind. Look at your fears and worries and try to dig a little deeper. Oftentimes there is something else beneath the surface. For example, we may fear failure, but when we ask ourselves why, we are likely to uncover a deeper fear, such as the fear of being seen as unworthy.

3. Do a reality check on these fears. Refer to Reality Testing (page 193) for this step. How many of these fears and worries are likely to come true?

4. Bring each and every one of your fears and worries to God in prayer. You can take some time to close your eyes and visualize yourself putting each fear and worry into

God's hands. You can physically make the motion of hand-ing each fear to the Lord.

5. Pray about each of your fears and worries throughout the week. At the end of the week, reflect on what God has shown you.

Tip

After Step 1, if you find that you're still feeling overwhelmed with emotions, take a break to do something that will help you feel more emotionally calm (e.g., see "Pick Me Up" List (page 205) before returning to this exercise.

ACTION PLANNING

Useful for: taking action when you feel anxiety, indecisiveness, lack of motivation

Time: 30–60 minutes, as often as needed

Experiencing fear and panic can paralyze our decision-making. If there is something that you have been feeling indecisive about, coming up with an action plan can help begin to alleviate some of your fears, worries, and indecisiveness.

---

1. Ask God to guide you as you come up with decisive actions and solutions to your current goals and challenges.

2. Choose something that you've been slow to act on or have been indecisive about.

3. Give yourself some time to check in with what's happening in your body. You can ask yourself the following:

   - What is it that I'm afraid of or trying to protect myself from?

   - What do I need in this moment?

4. Write down the obstacles, fears, or worries that are causing you to hesitate or be indecisive.

5. For each obstacle, fear, or worry, write down one or more small action step you can take.

6. Begin taking action toward addressing whatever is taking up most of your mental space.

Tip:

- It's completely okay if you can't think of anything tangible you can do to address a specific obstacle. If there is no clear action step, you can seek support from someone and pray for comfort, peace, and guidance.

- If taking action seems overwhelming, try breaking down the action step you came up with into an even smaller step. For example, put on a timer to commit to spending five minutes to work on the first step. Getting started is often the hardest part and starting with a small step can help you feel less overwhelmed.

INTENTIONAL ATTENTION

Useful for: being present with God and intentional with our attention

Time: 15 minutes, as often as needed

We are likely to react to external events because we get caught up with everything going on in our daily lives, making it difficult to stay present and intentional as we go about our day. A daily check-in can help us become more attuned with what is going on in our internal state.

Use this exercise to help carve out time to observe and reflect on where you've been focusing your time and attention. Get back to the present and connect with God every day.

Set an alarm or phone reminders for when you want to use this exercise.

---

1. Choose a Bible verse to meditate on during your check-ins.

2. When your alarm or reminder goes off, review the Bible verse you chose.

3. Check in with yourself to see what you're focused on. Here are some examples of things you can ask yourself:

   a. What is my attention focused on?

   b. What am I thinking and feeling?

   c. What is at least one thing I'd like to ask God for His help with?

4. After one week of daily check-ins, reflect on anything you observed or learned. Feel free to make adjustments that

will help you be more intentional about where your time and attention is focused.

Tip

If you find your time is too limited to complete the whole exercise, just choose one Bible verse or one thing from 3a to 3c to focus on during the check-in.

SET BOUNDARIES TO GUARD
YOUR MIND AND HEART

Useful for: stress management, overcoming burnout, work–life balance, improving relationships

Time: 30 minutes, as often as needed

When we've overloaded our plate and are on the brink of burnout, anxiety often flares. Sometimes it's easy to forget that we can take on too much of what might seem like a good thing (e.g., church activities, projects, social obligations). If we feel like we're being controlled by the demands of our workplace and people in our lives, we may be struggling with managing our time. It might be a sign that we've taken on too much and need additional support. Setting boundaries will help us prioritize and effectively steward our time and attention. When we examine the areas where we need boundaries, we are likely to discover that we have taken on roles that are not in the realm of our responsibility.

Boundaries can help us avoid bitterness and resentment in relationships and help us preserve our energy so that we can give our connections attention and care. Boundaries help us differentiate our responsibilities from other people's responsibilities. Boundaries are not about changing or controlling other people, but about taking personal responsibility for our choices and honestly acknowledging our limitations.

This exercise will give you an opportunity to come up with some boundaries so you can be a responsible steward and live purposefully as a vessel of God.

1. Write out the various areas of your life where you have responsibilities to fulfill (e.g., work, relationships, personal life, health, finances).

2. Write out what is causing you unnecessary stress and making it difficult to fulfill your responsibilities.

3. Look at whether you need to set boundaries in areas of your life. This might mean examining where you are saying yes to things when you could be saying no, or areas where it feels like you are taking on more than you can handle. Think of boundaries as a tool for stewarding your time so you can prioritize what God is asking you to focus on in this season.

4. Start with one thing you can do differently to establish boundaries. For example, you could decide not to take on any more projects until you've completed another project first. Boundaries can be related to time, physical space, and consequences related to how we are treated by others.

5. Write down your boundaries. Keep in mind boundaries are focused on your choices, actions, and responses. For example, "I have 30 minutes for our meeting today."

6. Clearly communicate your boundaries to relevant people, as applicable.

7. If your boundaries are not being respected, this is likely due to a lack of consistency or a limitation in others, not yourself. Keep a loving and graceful approach to reiterate your own limitations and why the boundary you're setting is important to you. Remind yourself that their response

is not your responsibility and that regardless of what they choose to do, you can still take responsibility for your own actions.

8. Feel free to readjust your boundaries periodically. They will need to change depending on circumstances and priorities. Continually ask God to help you determine what boundaries to set to help you be a more faithful steward.

Tip:

- Boundaries take practice and normally do not come naturally at first. If you're having trouble choosing what boundary to set, consider what it would cost you in the future if you choose not to set any boundaries in the areas you identified in Step 2. Assess and decide whether the cost (e.g., time, energy, rest) outweighs establishing a boundary.

- If you find yourself having trouble enforcing boundaries, it can be helpful to explore why it's difficult. Exploring our thoughts and feelings behind why it's hard for us to maintain boundaries can help us uncover thinking traps that we can dispel (see Explore Your Thoughts and Feelings (page 189), Faulty Thinking Traps (page 191), Reality Testing (page 193), Replace Lies and Meditate on Truths (page 194).

- You may be in a busy season where God's grace is especially needed. If you have set boundaries and still feel overloaded, it may be helpful to examine the areas where you may be relying on your strength alone, rather than God's grace. Oftentimes, God will pull us through difficult seasons in ways that only He can.

RECEIVING GOD'S LOVE AND COMPASSION

Useful for: overcoming self-condemnation, receiving God's love, embracing your identity in Christ

Time: 15 minutes

Sometimes we struggle to accept that God's love for us is personal. We may have taken on labels in our self-talk that don't reflect how God loves and views us. In our head, we can know that God's love is unconditional, while another part of us still believes we must earn God's love. God's love is so vast that it can be hard to imagine that God's love does not rely on anything you do for Him, but God is love and love defines who He is. This exercise will help you unlearn false labels and begin to accept and internalize God's love for you.

---

1. Observe your self-talk. If you've been keeping a thought journal, look for different things you have thought about yourself. What are the recurring themes or phrases?

2. Are there ways you've been putting yourself on a throne of condemnation, rather than on God's throne of grace? Are there things you've been telling yourself about your identity that are false labels (e.g., unworthy, broken, a hot mess)? Write each one on a separate piece of paper.

3. Bring each of these counterfeit identities to the throne of God's grace. You can tell God, *"I bring these labels, feelings, and thoughts to the throne of your grace. Please help me unlearn them and accept my true identity in Christ."*

4. Dispose the papers as you wish—you can crumple them up or rip them into pieces.

5. Meditate on the qualities of God's love. Try to open your heart to hear from God and be willing to receive and accept His love. Here are some examples of the attributes of God's love and relevant Scripture references:

   - God's love is unconditional. (Romans 8:38–39; John 6:37)

   - God's love is perfect and casts out fear. (1 John 4:18)

   - God's love is sacrificial. (John 15:13)

   - God's love never changes. (Isaiah 54:10)

   - God's love is everlasting. (James 1:17)

6. If there is any resistance to accepting God's love, take time to be still and observe. Acknowledge what is making it difficult. Share your observations with God. Ask God to remove these obstacles.

Tip:

- If you need a reminder of what your true identity in Christ is, review Identity-Based Scripture Declarations (page 178).

- Entertainment and media have twisted our perception and understanding of love. Review 1 Corinthians 13 to understand the meaning of love through a biblical lens. Be patient with yourself as you break down lies and learn the truth.

TAKING OFF YOUR MASKS

Useful for: improving relationships with God and others, living authentically and intentionally

Time: 20 minutes

Conforming is easy because we want to be accepted by people and avoid judgment and criticism. We put on certain masks to get people to like us or because we have learned what is expected of us. We try to keep up a façade. It's easier to pretend to be something we're not than to work on what needs to be changed.

God meets us where we are, not where we pretend to be. There may be certain things about ourselves that we don't like, but God doesn't want us to hide under a false pretense. We can bring those parts to Him so He can transform us from the inside out. This exercise will help you begin taking off the masks that are hindering you from coming to God in an honest and humble posture. God doesn't turn us away when we choose to be honest with Him.

---

1. Think about how you behave in different contexts and answer the following questions:

    - What is something you don't want others to know? Why?

    - What are you worried about that people would think of you?

    - Are there people in your life that you're afraid of disappointing?

- What are you afraid will happen if you disappoint someone?

- What are you afraid will happen if you're vulnerable?

- Are there certain masks you put on?

- What things do you do to mask feelings that you want to hide from others or even yourself?

- In what ways can you be more honest with yourself, others, and God?

2. Write down any masks that you have been putting on (e.g., perfect and put together, tough, independent, social butterfly, people pleaser). You can draw masks and label them to give you a visual to help you be more aware of them.

3. Ask God to help you take off each of the masks that have been hindering you from being your true self in Christ as He has made you.

4. Ask God to help you put on your true identity in Christ instead of the masks.

Tip:

- If you need a reminder of what your true identity in Christ is, review Identity-Based Scripture Declarations (page 178).

- There's nothing wrong with having certain personality traits that may incline us to be social butterflies or more independent, but what matters is how we choose to use them. We can ask God to help us use our unique personality traits for His glory, rather than to mask our true thoughts and feelings.

ANSWERED PRAYERS AND PRAISE REPORTS

Useful for: encouragement, overcoming unbelief, expressing gratitude

Time: Five mins, as often as needed

We tend to have a very short memory. We get easily discouraged when things don't seem to go our way and forget all
the times God has worked things out for the best. This is why
God calls us to walk by faith, and not by sight (2 Corinthians
5:7). This exercise will provide you with a tool that can help
remind you of all that God has already done in your life.
These reminders can give us hope and ground us in our faith.

---

1. Reflect and write down some things that God has done for
   you in your life.

2. Continue to keep a log of answered prayers and praise
   reports of things God has done in your life in a journal or
   on a note app in your phone. (Also refer to page 226 for
   prayers page.)

3. Revisit this log every time you need some encouragement
   and strength.

MEDITATE ON GOD'S NATURE AS OUR FATHER

Useful for: grounding yourself in your identity in Christ

Time: 10 minutes, as often as needed

God is a loving Father who has our best interests. He loves each one of us personally as His daughter and always keeps His promises. We are heirs to His kingdom. We can easily take these truths for granted. This exercise can remind you to relate to God as your Father and turn to Him as your main source of peace and comfort.

---

1. Ask the Holy Spirit to help you relate to God as His daughter. Allow yourself to sit in stillness with God for as long as you need.

2. Meditate on the following attributes of God as our Father. Look up any of the relevant Scriptures for evidence of these qualities.

   My heavenly Father:

   protects me (Psalm 18:2; 1 Corinthians 10:13)

   loves me (John 3:16; Romans 5:8)

   thinks of me and cares for me (Psalm 40:17; 1 Peter 5:7)

   supplies all my needs and more (Philippians 4:19; Ephesians 3:20)

   gives me rest (Matthew 11:28)

   gives me peace (Isaiah 26:3)

never changes
(Malachi 3:6)

never forsakes me
(Hebrews 13:5)

works for my good
in all circumstances
(Romans 8:28)

gives me wisdom
(James 1:5)

gives me the right words
to speak (Luke 12:12)

gives me joy (John 15:11)

sees my heart
(1 Samuel 16:7)

knows everything
(1 John 3:20)

disciplines me out of
love (Hebrews 12:6)

is merciful, patient,
gracious, and kind
(Ephesians 2:4–5;
Psalm 145:8–13)

is holy (Psalm 99:9)

3. Think about what it means to you that God is a loving Father. Is there anything that is making it difficult to view God in this way? If yes, talk to God about what is blocking you from receiving His love.

SEEING THE GOOD

Useful for: expressing gratitude, reframing challenges

Time: One to five minutes, as often as needed

As Christ followers, we have so much to be grateful for. We can be grateful that Jesus' death, burial, and resurrection led to the cleansing of our sins and saved us from the penalty of death. We can be grateful knowing that God has a home waiting for us in heaven (John 14:2–3).

Gratitude is not about bypassing our emotions or pretending everything is okay when it's not. It's about being able to identify the good even in the bad. The Bible says we can rejoice and "count it all joy" when we experience various temptations and trials (James 1:2–4). We can express gratitude for the lessons we learn and be thankful for our Father's correction (Job 5:17). Every trial and lesson we face helps us conform to the image of Jesus. Hardship strengthens our faith and helps us build character traits such as patience.

---

1. List challenges and obstacles that you are currently facing.

2. Ask God to help you see His grace in every situation and how He is using these challenges for your spiritual growth.

3. Write down what you can be thankful for in facing these challenges and obstacles (e.g., important lessons God is teaching you).

HEARING FROM GOD THROUGH SCRIPTURE

Useful for: connecting to God, experiencing comfort and peace, expressing gratitude

Time: 15 minutes, as often as applicable

In the past, you may have encountered a Scripture or read something from a devotional (maybe from this book!) that spoke directly to your heart and was relevant to a situation you were going through. This exercise will help you record these Scriptures so that you can be reminded of the times that God has spoken to you directly through His Word.

---

1. Select some of your favorite verses that have spoken to your heart and had an impact on your life.

2. In a journal or section of a journal, write down how each Scripture relates to you.

3. Reflect and write how God has used the verse to speak to you.

4. Look back at these reflections any time you need to be reminded and encouraged about God's faithfulness.

Tip

If you need guidance from God to make an important decision, ask Him to confirm it through Scripture. Check that your heart is yielded, open, and willing to do God's will.

LETTER WRITING

Useful for: conflict resolution, processing events and emotions

Time: 60 minutes, as often as needed

Reliving an event or planning a difficult conversation can keep us up at night. Perhaps someone hurt us, and we need to process our thoughts and feelings about the situation. Letter writing can be a great tool of expression.

---

1. Decide to whom you'll write. It can be someone who has hurt you, someone you've hurt, or someone you're trying to resolve a conflict with.

2. Here are some optional prompts to help kickstart your writing:

   - Write down what comes to mind when you think about the person you're writing to.

   - What would you like to express? What would you like them to understand or know? What would you like from this person moving forward?

   - What steps would help you to move forward?

   - What do you need to entrust to God?

3. Lean on what God wants you to do with the letter—throw it away, keep it for safekeeping, or send it to the person it's addressed to.

Prayers Answered

Record any reflections and insights you received in your prayer journey.

References

BOOKS

Anxiety Relief for Teens: Essential CBT Skills and Mindfulness Practices to Overcome Anxiety and Stress by Regine Galanti PhD

Boundaries: When to Say Yes, How to Say No to Take Control of Your Life by Henry Cloud and John Townsend

Lies Women Believe: And the Truth that Sets Them Free by Nancy Leigh DeMoss

Stand: Rising Up Against Darkness, Temptation, and Persecution by Marian Jordan Ellis

Tramp for the Lord by Corrie ten Boom

Her True Worth: Breaking Free from a Culture of Selfies, Side Hustles, and People Pleasing to Embrace Your True Identity in Christ by Brittany Maher and Cassandra Speer

When Strivings Cease: Replacing the Gospel of Self-Improvement with the Gospel of Life-Transforming Grace by Ruth Chou Simons

The Power of Habit: Why We Do What We Do in Life and Business by Charles Duhigg

Acknowledgements

I am thankful to my sister, Grace, my parents, my friends, and my church family for their love, prayers, input, support, and accountability. I am thankful to all my life coaching clients who have allowed me to support them on their journey, for which I am truly privileged and blessed. I would also like to thank Tahra Seplowin, Kim Suarez, Caroline Lee, and Megan Gerig, the editors at Penguin Random House for elevating my writing with their feedback, quality edits, and continual encouragement.

Above all, I am thankful to God for assigning me with this important task and equipping me to complete it.

About the Author

 **Helen H. Lee, MSc,** specializes in helping women experience a transformative relationship with God through Spirit-led coaching. Her passion is to help women learn to walk courageously in God's love and become who they are created to be so they can live their God-given purpose. Her coaching style is compassionate and client-centered and aimed at empowering clients to be led by the Holy Spirit and biblical principles so they can experience spiritual growth.

Helen is also a research consultant in psychology and works on projects supporting the Department of National Defence in Canada and is a PhD candidate in Industrial/Organizational Psychology at Western University.

Connect with Helen on Facebook or Instagram @grit.grace.grow.coaching.

Hi there,

We hope you enjoyed *Finding Peace: Prayer Journal for Women*. If you have any questions or concerns about your book, or have received a damaged copy, please contact customerservice@penguinrandomhouse.com. We're here and happy to help.

Also, please consider writing a review on your favorite retailer's website to let others know what you thought of the book!

Sincerely,
The Zeitgeist Team